A 52-WEEK DEVOTIONAL

Until Then

Journeying Between the Now and the Not Yet

By Michelle Adserias

PARENT COMPANY OF *TODAY'S CHRISTIAN LIVING*
TODAYSCHRISTIANLIVING.ORG

Until Then

Journeying Between the Now and the Not Yet
A 52-Week Devotional

Copyright © 2024

Published in Iola, Wisconsin by JP Media, LLC.

Photos by Michelle Adserias (except where credited).

All rights reserved. *Until Then: Journeying Between the Now and the Not Yet, A 52-Week Devotional* is under copyright protection. No part of this book may be used or reproduced in any manner whatsoever without written permission except in the case of brief quotations embodied in critical articles and reviews.

Unless otherwise noted, Scripture is taken from the
New King James Version © 1982 by Thomas Nelson.
Used with permission. All rights reserved.

THIS BOOK PRESENTED TO:

_____

BY

_____

ON

_____

INTRODUCTION

Before we are in Christ and He is in us, we live for ourselves. We do what we think is right or what feels right. If our values align with God's laws, sobeit. If not, well, that's okay too.

Then, if we are receptive, God opens our spiritual eyes. We realize our flesh is a fire-breathing dragon with an insatiable appetite — driven to attain all that glitters, even if it destroys us in the process. We understand we are on a trajectory to eternal death unless something changes — unless we change. Sadly, we are powerless to change ourselves. Just like Eustace, the boy-turned-dragon because of his own self-absorption in *The Voyage of the Dawn Treader* (C.S. Lewis), we realize we need to be rescued.

Praise God He sent His Son! When John the Baptist saw Jesus walking toward him in the wilderness, he announced — in a loud, confident voice — *"Behold! The Lamb of God who takes away the sin of the world!"* (John 1:39) Jesus came to our rescue by shedding His blood on the cross, a once-for-alll sin payment. Then He rose from the grave, defeating sin's penalty: death.

If we confess our sins, He is faithful and just to forgive us our sins and to cleanse us from all unrighteousness. (1 John 1:9)

At the moment we confess, as John Newton did, "I am a great sinner and Christ is a great Savior," putting our faith wholly in the Lamb of God who takes away the sins of the world, we are cleansed by Christ's blood and declared "not guilty." We are sealed with the Holy Spirit. We join God's family. Our new life as a new creation begins. We are saved (salvation).

Then we begin our spiritual journey toward Christlikeness. Although it's true we were saved by faith from our slavery to sin, we still dwell in our fire-breathing-dragon shells. We war with our flesh daily as we "work out our salvation with fear and trembling." Sin in us continues rearing its ugly head. Over time, Jesus patiently chips away at the vestiges of our old selves as we submit to His lordship and obediently follow Him.

It's not a pleasant process. It can be downright painful to allow God to rip sinful pleasures from our lives, even though we know they're destroying us. Eustace writhed when Aslan ripped away his dragon scales in long, painful strokes until the ugly, old creature was stripped away. It was all worthwhile when he emerged as a boy — and Aslan's friend. As we journey the twisted, gnarly path of life toward a closer friendship with our Savior, we are being saved (sanctification).

Our struggle will not end until we leave this earth behind and our souls find their final rest in the presence of God. Only then will our salvation be fully perfected. Our heart's desire to honor God in all we do, to walk with Him in untainted fellowship, will no longer be the hope sustaining us. It will be our forever reality. We will be complete in Christ and enjoy perfect fellowship with Him forever (glorification).

Beloved, now we are children of God; and it has not yet been revealed what we shall be, but we know that when He is revealed, we shall be like Him, for we shall see Him as He is. (1 John 3:2)

Once we are in Christ, we are not who we were before and still not all we will be. We are caught between what was and is yet to come. As we journey *"toward the goal for the prize of the upward call of God in Christ Jesus"* (Philippians 3:14), God is changing us, for our good and to His glory. The transformation others see in us isn't the result of our determination to be better people; it's the natural outcome of being in God's company, the fruit of the Spirit.

This journey we're on is not for the fainthearted. Sometimes we get tired. Sometimes the pain seems unbearable. Sometimes it costs us this world's comforts. Sometimes it costs us our lives. It's no wonder we are tempted, like the children of Israel begging to go back to slavery in Egypt, to turn around and go back to a more comfortable place despite the perils of sin's enslavement. But God asks us to endure "light, momentary afflictions" so He can refine us, bless us, and reveal Himself to us.

Our hearts and souls long to be with our heavenly Father in a place where suffering, striving, and sorrow are no more. That day will come. Until then, we are assigned the remarkable task of representing Him on earth, bringing Him glory through our words, our actions, and our attitudes.

I, therefore, the prisoner of the Lord, beseech you to walk worthy of the calling with which you were called, with all lowliness and gentleness, with longsuffering, bearing with one another in love, endeavoring to keep the unity of the Spirit in the bond of peace. (Ephesians 4:1-3)

ACKNOWLEDGEMENTS

Thank you to my publisher, Diana Jones, for making this devotional idea a reality.

I couldn't possibly name the countless people who taught me invaluable spiritual lessons along my journey from the now to the not yet — pastors, teachers, counselors and friends who have, by God's divine guidance, spoken the words I needed to hear when I needed to hear them.

This devotional was largely inspired by Reverend Richard Neale, the founder of Youth Gospel Crusade and Camp Forest Springs. In my mind's eye, I can see him teaching from a green, handmade wooden pulpit in the outdoor chapel — a series of wooden benches set into the hillside. The setting sun winks from the lake behind him while the white birch leaves clap and chatter in the breeze. I look forward to seeing him again in glory.

DEDICATION

This book is dedicated to my husband, Peter, who has always encouraged me to pursue what God calls me to do. I've never known a better man.

AUTHOR'S NOTE

Each week's devotional is freestanding. You can tackle the topics in any order you choose. My hope is to encourage you on your journey from salvation to glorification. Please use this tool as you see best.

UNTIL THEN

TABLE OF CONTENTS

JOURNEYING WITH GOD

Week 1: From Condemned to Redeemed

Week 2: From Death to New Life

Week 3: From Darkness to Light

Week 4: From Unclean to Holy

Week 5: From Impure to Purified

Week 6: From Scorn to Worship

Week 7: From Rebellion to Obedience

Week 8: From Fear to Peace

Week 9: From Apathy to Awe

Week 10: From Folly to Wisdom

Week 11: From Pride to Humility

Week 12: From Testing to Standing

Week 13: From Noise to Stillness

Week 14: From Seeking to Discovering

Week 15: From Wandering to Following

Week 16: From Flawed to Perfected

Week 17: From Goats to Sheep

Week 18: From Orphans to God's Children

Week 19: From Aliens to Citizens

Week 20: From Longing to Satisfaction

Week 21: From Waiting to Fulfillment

JOURNEYING WITH OTHERS

Week 22: From Rejection to Acceptance

Week 23: From Strangers to Family

Week 24: From Isolation to Fellowship

Week 25: From Many to One

Week 26: From Pretending to Authenticity

Week 27: From Judgment to Grace

Week 28: From Vengeful to Merciful

Week 29: From Unforgiving to Forgiving

Week 30: From Cruel to Kind

Week 31: From Selfish to Selfless

Week 32: From Sowing to Reaping

Week 33: From Serving to Being Served

Week 34: From Full Quiver to Empty Nest

Week 35: From Cursed to Blessed

Week 36: From Misunderstood to Fully Known

JOURNEYING WITH SELF

Week 37: From Conviction to Confession

Week 38: From Striving to Abiding

Week 39: From Busy to Restful

Week 40: From Aimless to Purposeful

Week 41: From Doubt to Security

Week 42: From Duty to Calling

Week 43: From Worry to Confidence

Week 44: From Uncertainty to Faith

Week 45: From Faithless to Faithful

Week 46: From Want to Plenty

Week 47: From Complaining to Contentment

Week 48: From Temporal to Eternal

Week 49: From Youth to Old Age

Week 50: From Mourning to Rejoicing

Week 51: From Defeat to Triumph

Week 52: From Discouragement to Hope

JOURNEYING WITH GOD (WEEKS 1-21)

It's impossible — yes, impossible — to please God without first being His redeemed child. Something marvelous, something beyond human comprehension, happens when we turn our backs on sin and self and we appeal to God's mercy and grace for forgiveness. When we accept God's free gift of salvation, everything changes — well, not the external, physical aspects of our circumstances, but the internal heart aspects are all made new.

We are newly indwelled by the Holy Spirit, who illumines the new book we live by, God's Word. Together they are a spiritual GPS, directing and guiding us through life. We have a new Father, a new family and a new eternal home. We have a new assignment that comes with new priorities. We have a new direction, new hope and a new outlook on life. We are new creations!

We gradually begin seeing the world as God sees it and seeing people through God's eyes. The more we surrender to God's will, the more we see our newness manifested in our daily lives. The more we obey His commands, the more we reflect our Savior to each other and to the world. We move from what was toward what is and what will be — someday.

WEEK 1: FROM CONDEMNED TO REDEEMED

CONSIDER:

Have you ever watched a meteor shower? I try to set aside one clear night each year to watch God's cosmic show. There are about 30 annually, all visible without using a telescope. The Perseid meteor shower, in mid-August, is the best. You can see 100 to 200 shooting stars per hour on a clear, moonless night.

Some shooters cruise across the star-studded speedway, quickly disappearing into the distant dark. Some stay on the horizon longer, going out with long tails blazing against blackness. Where they travel from, the things they've encountered along the way, and where their journeys will end, only their Creator knows.

Shooting stars aren't stars at all. They're bits of debris left behind by passing comets. As Earth orbits the sun, it passes through comet debris fields. When discarded pieces of comet, more commonly known as meteors, break through Earth's atmosphere, they quickly burn up — a brief white streak in the night sky.

Only God could make cosmic garbage into a shooting star. He transforms all the unwanted, unlovely fallout into something so awe-inspiring, people lay awake hoping to catch a glimpse of just one. We make wishes on them, write songs about them, and capture them on canvas.

In the course of a lifetime, we all accumulate refuse: a trail of broken promises, wrongs inflicted against God and others, unfulfilled hopes, tragic losses, injustices suffered. Some of it is beyond our control, but the unrepented sin warrants eternal condemnation. It builds a wall between us and God, one we can't scale. But when we repent — turn away from ourselves and toward God in mind, body, and heart — God forgives us. His love and grace envelope us. He redeems us.

There is therefore now no condemnation to those who are in Christ Jesus, who do not walk according to the flesh, but according to the Spirit. For the law of the Spirit of life in Christ Jesus has made me free from the law of sin and death. (Romans 8:1-2)

God intends to make something lovely out of the ugliest stuff in our lives. The road we each travel, the things we encounter along the way, and where our own journey on this earth will end, only the Creator knows.

Jan 1

WEEK 1

DAY 1 | PRAY:

All your paths, Lord, are mercy and truth, to those who keep your covenant and your testimonies. For your name's sake, Lord, forgive my sin, for it is great. Do not remember the sins of my youth and my rebellious ways. (Psalm 25)

DAY 2 | MEMORIZE:

Ephesians 1:7

*In Him we have redemption through His blood,
the forgiveness of sins, according to the riches of His grace.*

DAY 3 | READ AND RESPOND:

Genesis, Chapters 39-41

As young men, Joseph's brothers were jealous of Joseph and sold him into slavery. How did Joseph respond to his situation, even when things were dim?

Joseph responded with resilience and faith, choosing to trust God

Genesis 50:15-21.

How did God redeem the evils done against Joseph?

God meant it for good - many people should be kept alive

In what ways is Joseph's story a picture of God's coming redemption through His Son, Jesus?

Forgiveness

What difficult thing has God redeemed in your life? Can you trust Him to make something beautiful of it?

A period of depression and loneliness following a loss - led me to seek faith

WEEK 1

DAY 4 | DO:

Make plans to watch a meteor shower before the end of the year. You can do some internet research to find the best times and places to view meteor showers where you live. Allow yourself at least an hour or two to sit quietly (leave your electronics behind) and scan the skies for shooting stars.

REFLECTIONS

DAY 5 | JOURNAL:

Record prayers, thoughts or insights from your time with God.

WEEK 2: FROM DEATH TO NEW LIFE

CONSIDER:

Each season has its own personality and a unique appeal. I relish each one for different reasons, but spring is my favorite.

Some people find winter's grave, death-like stillness over the land depressing. Although I find the season's quiet refreshing, it can be bleak. The stripped-down trees look lifeless against the gray sky, hibernating creatures sleep in a near-morbid state in their dens, the dark hours linger in the morning and rush in at night, and it's cold. Ironically, it's even colder on clear days. The sun's warmth is so distant, it can't reach us.

Then, the Earth moves closer to the sun. Winter reluctantly succumbs to spring as the sun's palpable heat thaws its grip. The hibernators venture out. Tom turkeys strut their stuff for harems of hens while tomcats caterwaul like tortured, love-sick souls singing about their achy, breaky hearts. The birds, back from winter vacation, sing in the dawn. Every deciduous tree dons a new green robe. Sleepy roots send up fresh shoots. All that was gray and dormant is soon restored to full color and life.

Winter is a picture of our souls before Christ breathes new life into us. We are very much alive but go about our darkened days deprived of the light and life only God can offer. Then, if we listen to His voice, we will hear Him say,

Awake, you who sleep,
Arise from the dead,
And Christ will give you light. (Ephesians 5:14)

Spring is a picture of our spiritual rebirth. Apart from Christ, we are like living things under winter's dark tyranny. Though we were *"dead in your trespasses and sins"* (Ephesians 2:1), we are now *"alive to God in Christ Jesus."* (Romans 6:11) In *The Lion, the Witch and the Wardrobe*, C.S. Lewis chose unending winter to represent the White Witch's evil reign over Narnia and spring's return to represent Aslan's arrival — for good reasons. Life conquers death. Light triumphs over darkness.

We awaken from spiritual slumber to a new life full of the spiritual riches God lavishes on us. (Ephesians 1:3-10 and 1 John 3:1, NIV) He cloaks us in a new robe of righteousness, purchased and freely given by Jesus Himself. He gives life true meaning. We are reborn to an eternal purpose. Is there anything better to live for?

WEEK 2

DAY 1 | PRAY:

I have sinned greatly in what I have done. Now, Lord, I beg you, take away the guilt of your servant. I have done a very foolish thing. (2 Samuel 24)

DAY 2 | MEMORIZE:

2 Corinthians 5:17 (ESV)

Therefore, if anyone is in Christ, he is a new creation. The old has passed away. Behold, the new has come.

DAY 3 | READ AND RESPOND:

Colossians 3:5-17

What are the traits of our old, wintery selves we must put off?

anger, rage, malice, slander, filthy language

What are the traits of our new selves we must put on?

Being renewed in knowledge in the image of its creator

What is the most important thing we must put on? How does that impact our relationship with God and others?

Have compassion, kindness, humility, gentleness and patience

What does this passage have to say about being at peace with God?

Be thankful

Let the peace of Christ rule in your heart

DAY 4 | DO:

Read *The Lion, the Witch and the Wardrobe* by C.S. Lewis. (It's a quick read.) Consider the ways this story parallels the gospel story. Is there something in particular that stands out to you in this book?

REFLECTIONS

DAY 5 | JOURNAL:

Record prayers, thoughts, or insights from your time with God.

WEEK 3: FROM DARKNESS TO LIGHT

CONSIDER:

I impose my fascination with caves on my family regularly. On every cave tour we've been on, the guide douses the lights at some point. Profound darkness settles in. It's a little unnerving.

When we visited Jewel Cave, the guide told us about a young man who led lantern-light tours there in the 1800s. On one trip, he was intrigued by a new passage. He asked his group to wait while he took the lantern and explored. Apparently, he found another route out of the cave, went home, and had a good night's sleep. The next morning, he realized he'd left his group in the cave all night — without any light. Can you imagine being trapped by complete darkness?

Without the light of Christ, we flounder in profound spiritual darkness. Like the tour-takers left in the cave, we can't make out the path ahead. Any attempt to find our own way leaves us in grave danger.

Acts 9 records Paul's encounter with Jesus on the Damascus road. Jesus was sending Paul to the Gentiles *"to open their eyes, in order to turn them from darkness to light, and from the power of Satan to God, that they may receive forgiveness of sins and an inheritance among those who are sanctified by faith in Me."* (Acts 26:18)

Christ opens our eyes when we follow Him. Jesus, the light, drives out spiritual darkness so we can see the path ahead — and lead others to the light of the world.

> *You are the light of the world. A city that is set on a hill cannot be hidden. Nor do they light a lamp and put it under a basket, but on a lampstand, and it gives light to all who are in the house. Let your light so shine before men, that they may see your good works and glorify your Father in heaven.* (Matthew 5:14-16)

Here's the interesting thing about darkness and light: Darkness is the absence of light, so light can drive out darkness. Imagine how excited those abandoned spelunkers were to see the light from their guide's lantern grow brighter with each step he took toward them!

Darkness, on the other hand, can never drive out light. Jesus came to earth *"to give light to those who sit in darkness and the shadow of death, to guide our feet into the way of peace."* (Luke 1:79) His indelible light gives us spiritual understanding and illumines our pathway to God.

DAY 1 | PRAY:

For with you is the fountain of life. In your light I see light. Continue your love to me. Your love, Lord, reaches to the heavens, your faithfulness to the skies. (Psalm 36)

DAY 2 | MEMORIZE:

John 8:12

Then Jesus spoke to them again, saying, "I am the light of the world. He who follows Me shall not walk in darkness, but have the light of life."

DAY 3 | READ AND RESPOND:

John 1:1-10

What two names is Jesus given in this passage?

The Word & The light

John notes that all creation came into being through Christ, first in verse 3 and then again in verse 10, where he goes on to say the world did not recognize its creator. What point do you think John is trying to make?

The world did not understand the true identity and power of their creator

Why did the world not recognize Him?

spiritual blindness
People chose darkness over the light of Jesus

According to 2 Corinthians 11:12-15, who disguises himself as an angel of light, and why must we be aware of his schemes?

Satan disguises himself
This deception allows him to appear good and truthful, making it easier to mislead people

DAY 4 | DO:

You'll need a candle (preferably a taper candle in a candleholder), a bright lamp or flashlight, and a dark room. In the dark room, light your candle and put it near the wall. Now, shine a bright light on the candle so it casts a shadow on the wall. Do you notice anything curious about the shadow? How does this relate to the truth that darkness cannot overcome light?

REFLECTIONS

DAY 5 | JOURNAL:

Record prayers, thoughts, or insights from your time with God.

WEEK 4: FROM UNCLEAN TO HOLY

CONSIDER:

Pigs get a bad rap. It's true — they wallow in mud and are sloppy critters. Their mud baths, however, serve a vital purpose. Pigs get overheated because they have fewer sweat glands and more fat than most animals. A good roll in the muck cools them off and keeps them comfortable as the water evaporates off their bodies. They're doing what their Creator intended.

Unclean living in people was never God's intent. He created Adam and Eve so He could enjoy their company. He blessed and cared for them. In those early Garden of Eden days, they all walked together in perfect fellowship. Sin's uncleanness was introduced by Eve's willingness to listen to Satan and Adam's willingness to follow Eve's lead. Their sin made perfect fellowship with God impossible. We mustn't be too hard on our ancestors, though. We would've done the same thing if we were in their bare feet.

The gospel's beautiful message is this: We don't have to wallow in sin's mud forever.

But if we walk in the light as He is in the light, we have fellowship with one another, and the blood of Jesus Christ His Son cleanses us from all sin. (1 John 1:7)

We can't go on garden walks with God on this side of heaven, but we can enjoy His fellowship. Christ made the impossible possible when He paid sin's price on the cross — and defeated death, sin's penalty. When we put our faith in Christ alone, we trade our sin (and its penalty) for Christ's righteousness.

Because of this Great Exchange, God sees us as holy even though we're trapped in our sin-riddled shells until physical death. Still, Paul makes it clear in Romans we are no longer slaves to sin. We are free in Christ.

That does not mean we are free to live as we please. We have a divine assignment: to live holy lives by the power of the Holy Spirit who lives in us. We're set apart for God's purposes. To be holy is to be keenly aware we are God's ambassadors on earth — to choose what is good, and right, and pure, and God-honoring. He has appointed us to proclaim, through our words and actions, God's praises as we *"walk worthy of the Lord, fully pleasing Him, being fruitful in every good work and increasing in the knowledge of God."* (Colossians 1:10)

WEEK 4

DAY 1 | PRAY:

Create in me a clean heart, O God, and renew a steadfast spirit within me. Do not cast me away from your presence, and do not take your Holy Spirit from me. Restore to me the joy of your salvation, and renew a right spirit in me. (Psalm 51)

DAY 2 | MEMORIZE:

1 Peter 1:15-16

But as He who called you is holy, you also be holy in all your conduct, because it is written, "Be holy, for I am holy."

DAY 3 | READ AND RESPOND:

1 Peter 1:13-25

We're given some instructions to help us be holy as God is holy. What are they?

Don't be influenced by worldly distractions. Reject old sins - pursue a life that reflects God's character.

Why should we live our lives with fear (awe/respect) for the Lord?

Fearing the Lord will give you wisdom.

What is one outward sign we are living holy lives?

praying
attending church
demonstrating acts of kindness

How long will God's Word endure? How does knowing this truth make you feel?

God's word endures forever!!
secure, comforted, hopeful

DAY 4 | DO:

Pick or buy a flower and put it in a vase. Try to check on it every day and make note of when it begins to fade and when it dies. Allow it to remind you how brief life is and to live for eternal things.

REFLECTIONS

DAY 5 | JOURNAL:

Record prayers, thoughts, or insights from your time with God.

WEEK 5: FROM IMPURE TO PURIFIED

CONSIDER:

On my first backpacking venture in the Porcupine Mountains, I thought nothing of drinking straight from the streams and rivers. Unlike the Wisconsin River, which ran through my hometown, these waterways sparkled clean and pure as they rushed over the rocks toward Lake Superior, inviting me to savor their cold refreshment.

Then I learned about giardia. Giardia is a microscopic parasite that does messy things to your digestive system. Since animals aren't terribly discriminating about where they relieve themselves, it's not uncommon for giardia to be swimming around in even the most pristine-looking waters. I don't drink directly from streams anymore. I purify the water first.

The Bible doesn't discuss purifying water, but it does make reference to purifying gold. In biblical times, the only method for refining gold was melting it in a fire. The gold sank to the bottom and the impurities rose to the top, where they were skimmed away. The process tested the authenticity of the gold and removed anything that diminished its value.

God puts us through fiery trials not only to test the authenticity of our faith but to bring all the impurities in our lives to the surface, where He can skim them off and throw them away.

Pure gold has a quality that is both a blessing and a curse. It's very soft. On the downside, it's easily damaged. On the upside, it's malleable. Testing and trials often leave us with wounds. They also make it easier for our Father to mold us into the image of Jesus.

Enduring trials can range on a scale from unpleasant to life-altering, from uncomfortable to grievous, so 1 Peter 1:6-7 offers these encouraging words:

In this you greatly rejoice, though now for a little while, if need be, you have been grieved by various trials, that the genuineness of your faith, being much more precious than gold that perishes, though it is tested by fire, may be found to praise, honor, and glory at the revelation of Jesus Christ.

In the words of the *Westminster Shorter Catechism*, "The chief end of man is to glorify God and enjoy Him forever." Our earthly testing will be found to God's glory when Christ is revealed as King of kings and Lord of lords. And, when all of life's trials are a distant memory, we will be eternally purified and enjoy Him forever in His perfect kingdom.

WEEK 5

DAY 1 | PRAY:

For you, God, tested me. You refined me as silver is refined. I went through fire and through water, but you brought me out to rich fulfillment. I bless you, O God. You have not turned away my prayer nor your mercy from me! (Psalm 66)

DAY 2 | MEMORIZE:

1 Peter 4:16

Yet if anyone suffers as a Christian, let him not be ashamed, but let him glorify God in this matter.

DAY 3 | READ AND RESPOND:

Job 21:1-17

Job is in the middle of a horrendous trial. What are his complaints in verses 1-7? What can we learn from this?

_____
_____
_____

Why is Job confident he will come through this trial with God's blessings in verses 8-12?

They should not fear God

In verses 13-17, why does Job fear God? How do the previous verses balance out Job's fear?

God is always present

Have you ever felt, like Job did, that God was nowhere to be found?

_____
_____

WEEK 5

DAY 4 | DO:
Find a Bible verse that confirms God is with us in our trials.

REFLECTIONS

Psalm 91:15

God will call upon me and I will answer him
I will be with him in trouble
I will rescue him and honor him

DAY 5 | JOURNAL:
Record prayers, thoughts, or insights from your time with God.

Thank you Lord for always being there for me - in times of trouble, fear, anxiety, and pain - You are an awesome God ♥ - Amen!!

WEEK 6: FROM SCORN TO WORSHIP

CONSIDER:

What do C.S. Lewis, Lee Strobel, and Josh McDowell have in common? They were all skeptics who set out to disprove the Bible. They scorned what God calls "truth." They rejected Him and disregarded His people. Determined to silence the church, they researched, read, and reasoned. The more they learned, the more convinced they were that God, in fact, does exist.

In their sincere search for truth, each man had an unexpected encounter with the Living God. He opened their spiritual eyes. How do you suppose they reacted when they realized they were wrong? I don't like being wrong. I doubt they liked it either. I imagine they all wrestled with God before admitting defeat.

We shouldn't be surprised by their spiritual awakening. God promised, *"You will seek me and find me when you search for Me with all your heart."* (Jeremiah 29:13) God opened their eyes to see the wondrous things He has done. He gave these former scorners a new name: worshippers. They were once at odds with God. Now they live at peace with Him.

They're in good company. Saul set out to silence the church. Convinced Jesus was a heretic and His followers a threat to Jewish society, he tracked down and imprisoned Christians. Unlike the three great leaders of our day, Saul wasn't actively seeking the truth. He was zealously trying to suppress it, convinced his actions were righteous.

One day, he was walking along, minding his own business, when he had an unexpected encounter with the Living God. Jesus blinded Saul with His Shekinah glory and asked a straightforward question: "Why are you persecuting Me, Saul?" Saul never answered the question.

He was physically blinded for a few days but Saul's spiritual eyes were opened. God changed him from a scoffer to a worshipper and gave him a new name: Paul. (Acts 13) God's adversary became His ally.

When we worship, we elevate God to His proper place in our hearts. We proclaim His worthiness to receive all *"power and riches and wisdom and strength and honor and glory and blessing."* (Revelation 5:12) But worship is more than lifting our hands and voices in praise. We demonstrate His worthiness when we submit to the King of king's lordship. Romans 12:1 refers to obedient, sacrificial living as our *"true and proper worship."* (NIV) Or, as James put it, *"Faith without deeds is useless."* (James 2:20, NIV)

WEEK 6

DAY 1 | PRAY:

You are worthy, O Lord, to receive glory and honor and power; for you created all things, and by your will they exist and were created. (Revelation 4)

DAY 2 | MEMORIZE:

Psalm 95:6-7a

Oh come, let us worship and bow down;
Let us kneel before the Lord our Maker.
For He is our God,
And we are the people of His pasture,
And the sheep of His hand.

DAY 3 | READ AND RESPOND:

Acts 9:1-21

On the road to Damascus, why did Saul fall down trembling when he saw the light of God's glory? What can we learn from this?

He heard Jesus ask him why do you persecute me

Why did Jesus ask Saul "Why are you persecuting Me?" rather than "Why are you persecuting My church?"

Because the church is considered the body of Christ, and essentially harming Jesus himself

What did Saul ask Jesus after He revealed Himself?

Who are you, Lord

What evidence do we see of a sincere change in Saul from scorner to worshipper?

He began speaking the truth about Jesus

DAY 4 | DO:

Take time this week to bow before God and worship Him. Ask Him how you can demonstrate your worshipful heart through your actions. Offer yourself as a living sacrifice. Warning: Living sacrifices can crawl off the altar.

REFLECTIONS

DAY 5 | JOURNAL:

Record prayers, thoughts, or insights from your time with God.

WEEK 7: FROM REBELLION TO OBEDIENCE

CONSIDER:

I marveled over the beauty and destructive force of an ice storm that moved through. The ice left every tree, every fence post, every rooftop shimmering like glass. Tall, slender white pines bowed toward silver-struck maples, then took up a graceful dance to the wind's somber music. The colliding limbs clattered like Christmas lights hitting the hardwood floor. It was an eerie sound. Sadly, many of those branches broke under the weight of their eye-catching burden.

Destructive sins often come wrapped in shimmering packages. For me, it's those ever-tempting chocolates in colorful foil, games with flashing lights calling you to play one more time, and racks of clothes I don't really need with big 75% Off signs on them. Whatever sins we fall prey to, they wreak havoc on our bodies, minds, and souls.

When we break under the burden of our sin-bents, we dance to the music of temptation and are subject to its destructive forces. Since we are powerless to escape sin's icy bonds on our own, the best thing we can do is avoid it — at all costs. In fact, the Bible instructs us to run! Run like Joseph did when Potipher's wife tried to seduce him.

Obedience is outward, empirical evidence we're being transformed by His radical love. God commands the wind and the rain. They obey. God also commands us. Unlike the wind and the rain, we can choose whether to obey. By choosing obedience, we demonstrate our love for God, just as Christ's obedience to death on the cross demonstrated His love for us. (Philippians 2:8)

For this is the love of God, that we keep His commandments. And His commandments are not burdensome. (1 John 5:3)

Sometimes God's commands seem burdensome. Not only burdensome — impossible! How can we love our enemies? How can we forgive those who hurt or disappoint us? How can we leave our comfort zone to serve God somewhere foreign to us? How can we stand for Christ, even if it costs us our lives? There's only one answer to such questions:

For the love of Christ compels us, because we judge thus: that if One died for all, then all died; and He died for all, that those who live should live no longer for themselves, but for Him who died for them and rose again. **(2 Corinthians 5:14-15)**

DAY 1 | PRAY:

Teach me the way of your statutes, Lord, and I will keep them to the end. Give me understanding, and I will keep your law; I will observe it with my whole heart. (Psalm 119)

DAY 2 | MEMORIZE:

Psalm 119:44-45

So shall I keep Your law continually,
Forever and ever.
And I will walk at liberty,
For I seek Your precepts.

DAY 3 | READ AND RESPOND:

Acts 15:12-42

What price were the apostles willing to pay for their obedience to God and His work?

Potentially facing opposition and conflict from Jews

Did they view their obedience, and the price they paid for it, as a burden?

No - they viewed them as Necessary

Have you ever paid a price for your obedience to God? What did it cost you?

Sacrificing personal comfort.

How does denying sin and obeying Christ allow you to walk at liberty?

Accepting Jesus Christ as your savior, you are essentially freed from the bondage of sin

DAY 4 | DO:

Write down one of God's commands you have trouble following. Ask God for the desire and power to obey it. Over time, do you notice any changes in that area of your life? Be gracious to yourself! They can be small changes.

REFLECTIONS

DAY 5 | JOURNAL:

Record prayers, thoughts, or insights from your time with God.

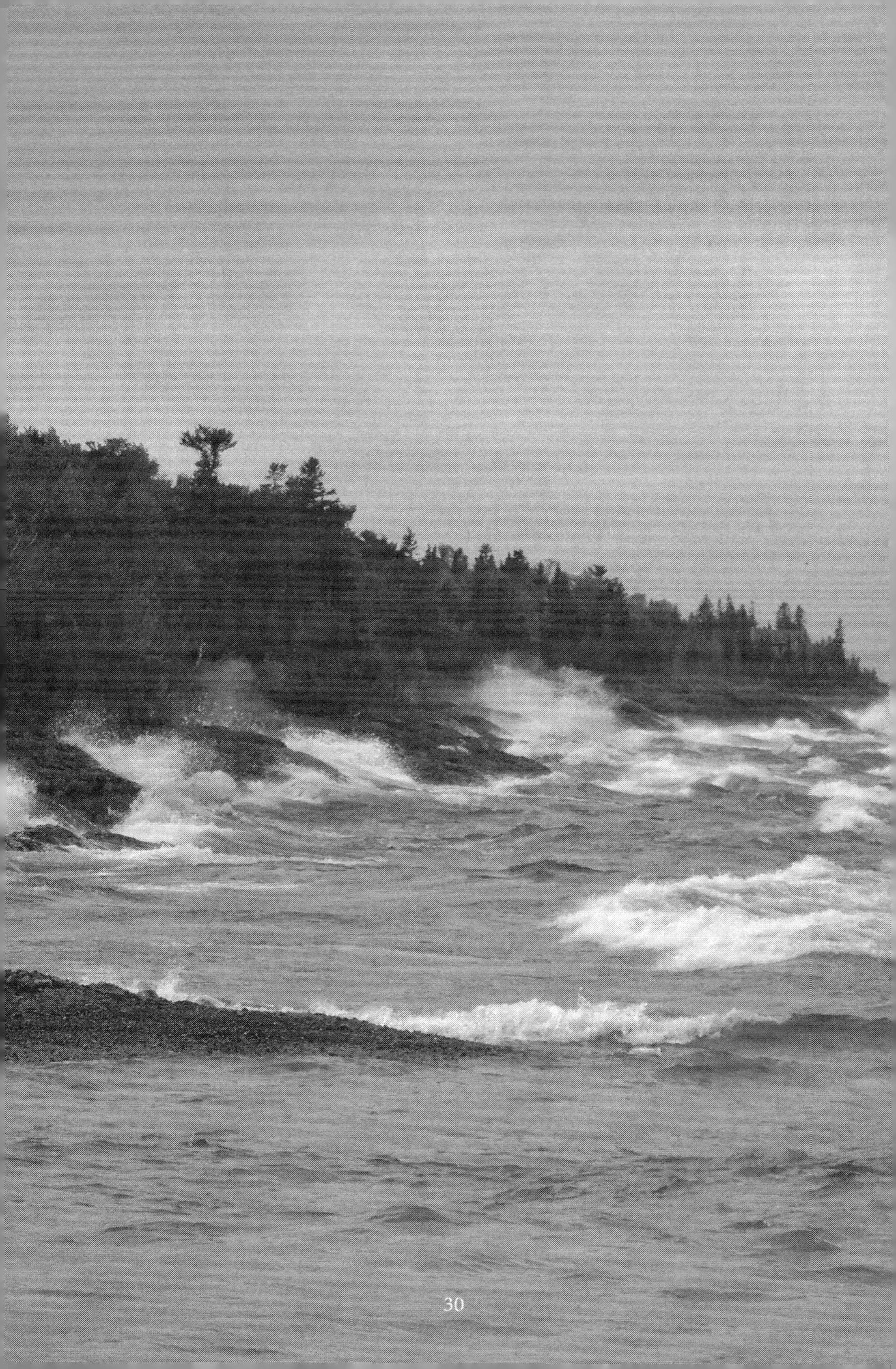

WEEK 8: FROM FEAR TO PEACE

CONSIDER:

Are you naturally drawn to water? I know I am. There's a reason for that. Scientists agree listening to waves sifting the sandy beach, or rivers clamoring and careening over slabs of bedrock, feeds our creativity, calms our minds. and refreshes us — body and soul. Why? No one is certain, but some evidence suggests the natural sounds of moving water cause a chemical change in our brains that makes us happier and healthier.

As soothing as it can be, water is also a powerful force that warrants our respect. Even easy-going rivers and relatively gentle waves have enough force to prod and push us along with their currents. I've spent enough time sitting in a canoe, grounded on a rock in the middle of the river, to know this is true. And when floodwaters rise, hurricanes kick up, or tsunamis strike, our healthy respect can escalate to gut-level fear. Water can be destructive. Water can be life-threatening.

For those outside God's family, He is to be feared like a tsunami. His innate justice and holiness demand eternal death for anyone who rejects His saving grace. But God's adopted children exchange the terror of God's wrath for the rightful respect due a loving Heavenly Father.

God's love is a never-ending river of rich mercy, divine righteousness, and perfect peace. His living waters are limitless, flowing unabated toward all who welcome His love. There are no breaks, no pauses, no hints of hesitation as more and more pours out from His limitless storehouse. Since we know nothing *"shall be able to separate us from the love of God which is in Christ Jesus our Lord"* (Romans 8:38-39), we don't need to fear God's judgment. We only need fear Him in the sense of giving Him the honor He is due. We can rest in God's perfect love and find perfect peace.

Love has been perfected among us in this: that we may have boldness in the day of judgment; because as He is, so are we in this world. There is no fear in love; but perfect love casts out fear, because fear involves torment. But he who fears has not been made perfect in love. We love [Him] because He first loved us. (1 John 4:17-19)

WEEK 8

DAY 1 | PRAY:

I will be secure, because there is hope in you. I will look about and take my rest in safety. I will lie down, with no one to make me afraid. I will forget my trouble, recalling it only as waters gone by. (Job 11)

DAY 2 | MEMORIZE:

John 14:27

Peace I leave with you, My peace I give to you; not as the world gives do I give to you. Let not your heart be troubled, neither let it be afraid.

DAY 3 | READ AND RESPOND:

Joshua 1:1-9

As God is sending Joshua across the Jordan River into the Promised Land, how many times does He instruct Joshua to be strong and courageous?

three times

According to Numbers 13:38, what do Joshua and the Israelites have to fear in their new land?

the people in the land were too strong to conquer

Why doesn't Joshua need to be afraid?

God repeatedly tells him to be strong and courageous assuring him that he will be with him wherever he goes.

What specific instructions and promises does God give Joshua in verses 7-8?

Be strong and courageous, meditate on the book of the law day and night and do everything written in it.

DAY 4 | DO:

Set aside half an hour to sit on the shore of a river, lake, or ocean. (No, running water from your faucet does not count.) Listen to the sounds of moving water. Do you notice any changes in your stress level? Your mood? Did God bring anything special to mind during this quiet time?

REFLECTIONS

DAY 5 | JOURNAL:

Record prayers, thoughts, or insights from your time with God.

(Photo credit © [Kenneth Keifer] / Adobe Stock)

WEEK 9: FROM APATHY TO AWE

CONSIDER:

Do you ever read a Bible passage and ask yourself, "What in the world does *that* mean?" I came across this one in Zephaniah 1:12 (KJV):

And it shall come to pass at that time, that I will search Jerusalem with candles, and punish the men that are settled on their lees: that say in their heart, "The Lord will not do good, neither will he do evil."

What are lees and how do men settle on them?

Lees are what we would call dregs. It's the organic sediment that forms in the bottom of a wine bottle during the fermentation process. Letting wines "settle on their lees" initially adds flavor to the wine. But if the wine is undisturbed for too long, the lees will spoil it. It needs to be strained and poured into a clean bottle from time to time, to preserve its flavor.

Settling on our lees is like resting on our laurels. Content with past victories, we can become complacent toward God and our assignment from Him. Instead of joining in the race, we set up our lawn chairs along the course and cheer the runners along. While encouraging others is a good thing, it's far more powerful to run alongside someone.

No sincere believer pursues apathy. Our hearts are simply distracted from godly pursuits. Sin creeps in and dulls the Holy Spirit's voice. It takes intentional effort to regularly reorient our hearts toward God, to pour our wine into fresh bottles so we won't be spiritually ruined.

In Romans 12:9, Paul instructs the church: *"Abhor what is evil. Cling to what is good."* Those are strong verbs instructing us to turn against sin and pursue righteousness.

How do we reignite a sense of awe when apathy settles in? It requires a heart adjustment. God begins making our sojourn in sin uncomfortable, even painful. *"For whom the Lord loves He chastens, and scourges every son whom He receives."* (Hebrews 12:6) He stirs our souls. Our part is to turn around and walk back toward God. As we pursue Him once again, we hear the Holy Spirit's still, small voice guiding, convicting, and comforting us once again.

When we look into the depths of our own depravity, we see the unlimited depths of God's unfailing love toward His undeserving children. God forgives and restores us over and over again. Hallelujah!

Great is the Lord and greatly to be praised, and His greatness is unsearchable.
(Psalm 145:3)

WEEK 9

DAY 1 | PRAY:

Restore me, God my Savior, and let go of your displeasure toward me. Revive me again, that I may rejoice in you. Show me your unfailing love, Lord, and grant me your salvation. (Psalm 85)

DAY 2 | MEMORIZE:

Hebrews 12:28 (NASB1995)

Therefore, since we receive a kingdom which cannot be shaken, let us show gratitude, by which we may offer to God an acceptable service with reverence and awe.

DAY 3 | READ AND RESPOND:

Revelation 3:14-21

What message does Jesus have for the church of Laodicea in verses 15-16?

He assures them that he will not let anyone "shut the door" on their opportunity to spread the Gospel

Because the people are living in spiritual apathy, what has happened to them?

They have become complacent and self-satisfied with their spiritual state

What does Jesus advise them to do?

Repent and become spiritually zealous – buy righteousness and spiritual insight

What promise does He give to those who overcome?

They will be granted the right to sit with him on his throne

WEEK 9

DAY 4 | DO:

Choose one aspect of God's character that awes you. This week, watch for ways God demonstrates that characteristic in your day-to-day life. Write them in your journal and praise God for them.

REFLECTIONS

God is omnipotence, omnipresence, omniscience and holiness

DAY 5 | JOURNAL:

Record prayers, thoughts, or insights from your time with God.

(Photo credit: © Jimj / Adobe Stock)

WEEK 10: FROM FOLLY TO WISDOM

CONSIDER:

One night, when I was in college, the northern lights were beyond beautiful — they were spectacular. A cone of red light hung directly overhead, suspended from the heavens. Pinpoints of white starlight pierced through translucent clouds of light dancing across the far reaches of the Milky Way, undulating and pulsating in great waves. An occasional beam, like a cosmic spotlight, would slowly grow, then disappear into the same mysterious nothingness from which it came. Each graceful movement was a new step in the heavenly ballet.

It's hard to witness such a grand display and doubt the power and abundant goodness of God — yet many credit it to a big bang and a bunch of freak accidents. By denying God's existence, they extinguish an inborn knowing that an incomprehensible, inexplicable power set the universe in motion. They trade God's wisdom for man's.

Here's what Paul said about human wisdom in 1 Corinthians 3:18-19:

Let no one deceive himself. If anyone among you seems to be wise in this age, let him become a fool that he may become wise. For the wisdom of this world is foolishness with God. For it is written, "He catches the wise in their own craftiness."

The secular world labels us fools for following an unseen Savior. I suppose it does seem strange for us to believe in someone intangible. Still, we see His reflection in all the wonders He created. We see His hand in the miraculous things He does. Whatever the world may think, I'd rather be a fool for Christ and wise in God's eyes.

God's life-giving wisdom is readily available to anyone who desires it. James 1:5 promises:

But if any of you lacks wisdom, let him ask of God, who gives to all generously and without reproach, and it will be given to him.

Don't hesitate to ask! And how can we know our wisdom is from God, not from this world? James goes on to say,

The wisdom that is from above is first pure, then peaceable, gentle, willing to yield, full of mercy and good fruits, without partiality and without hypocrisy. (James 3:17)

The wisdom God gives us, divinely guided wisdom, is consistent with His character. When our decisions or actions are not marked with purity, peace, gentleness, humility, mercy, impartiality, and authenticity, we can be sure we're exercising worldly wisdom, AKA foolishness.

WEEK 10

DAY 1 | PRAY:

Lord, give me a discerning heart, so I can distinguish between good and evil. Help me search for understanding as silver and seek for it as a hidden treasure, so I can understand what it means to know you and fear you. (1 Kings 3, Proverbs 1)

DAY 2 | MEMORIZE:

Proverbs 3:13-14

Happy is the man who finds wisdom,
And the man who gains understanding;
For her proceeds are better than the profits of silver,
And her gain than fine gold.

DAY 3 | READ AND RESPOND:

Proverbs 3

In verses 7-8, why should we not be wise in our own eyes? What keeps us from becoming prideful?

_____
_____

Verses 13-18 list some of the benefits of finding wisdom.

_____
_____
_____

What advice does Solomon offer about interacting with others in verses 27-30?

_____
_____
_____

In the final verse of this chapter, Solomon talks about the legacy we will leave behind. How do you want to be remembered?

_____
_____

DAY 4 | DO:

This week, do something nice for someone you don't know very well — a neighbor, a coworker, maybe a clerk or barista at a place you frequent. Be creative! It doesn't have to be extravagant.
Any small, unexpected act of kindness will do.

REFLECTIONS

DAY 5 | JOURNAL:

Record prayers, thoughts, or insights from your time with God.

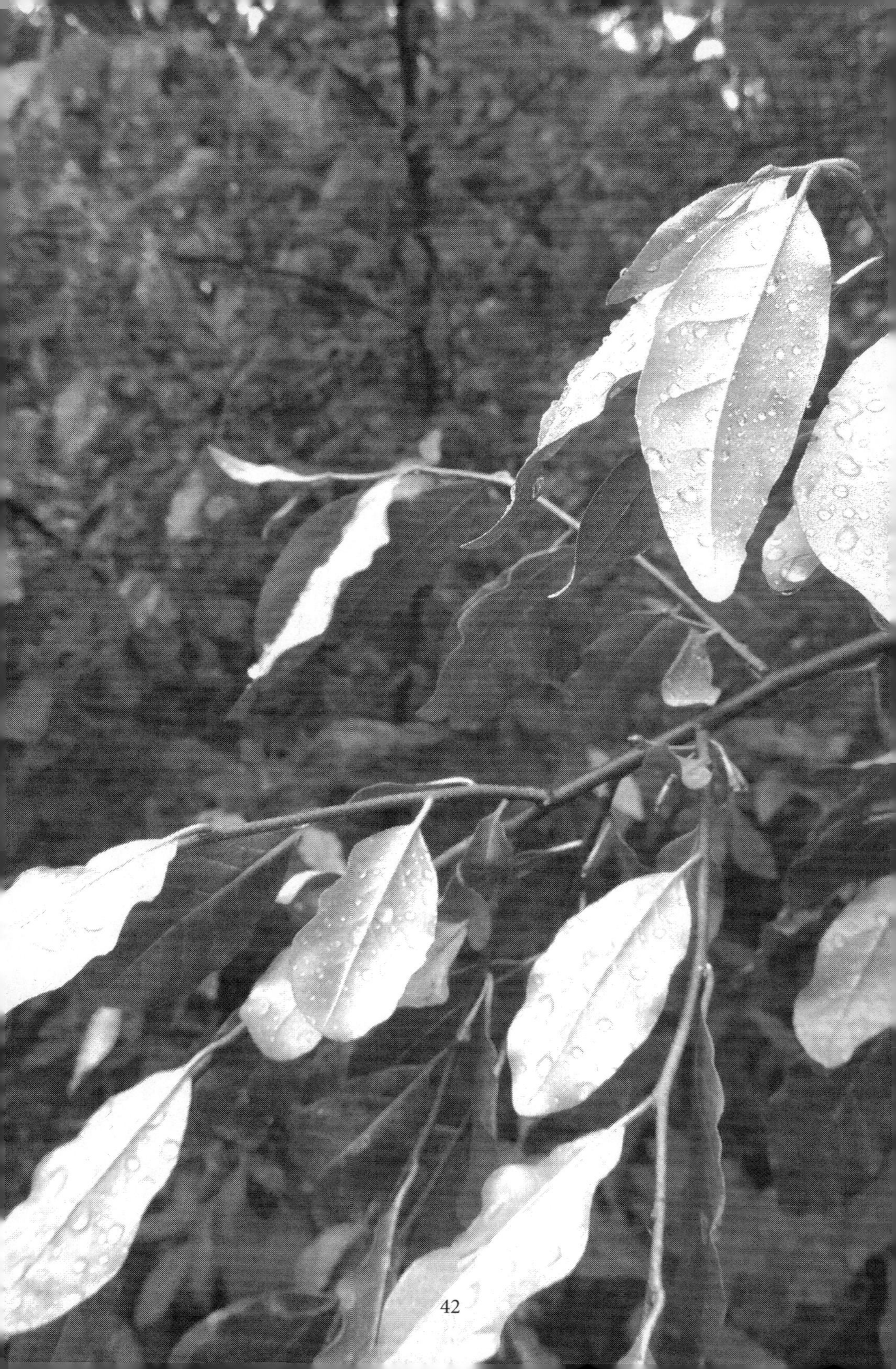

WEEK 11: FROM PRIDE TO HUMILITY

CONSIDER:

Every leaf has two sides: the darker, glossy side we see trees lifting up to the sunlight on pleasant days and the lighter, matte underside. The rich color on the greener side, which typically faces the sun, is richer in chlorophyll. The glossy surface seems to offer protection from excessive heat and destructive insects.

Have you noticed the leaves on certain trees flip over before it rains? Their high-gloss surfaces bow toward the ground, revealing their matte underside. Maple leaves are particularly striking in this pose because of their silver hue.

There's a reason the leaves behave differently before it rains. Here's how the *Old Farmer's Almanac* explains it:

Before a cold front arrives with its clouds and rains, the wind is often from the southwest. With the wind in this direction, the plant or tree orients itself to get optimum sunlight, and the leaves are in an unstable position with respect to the wind moving past them. This instability makes the leaves flip over. The unstable leaves then foretell the approach of a cold front which is likely to bring rain.

The leaves have a lesson for us. Being oriented to God's light is a wonderful thing. But it can leave us unstable. How is that possible? Shouldn't we be *more* stable when we reach to know more about God and know God more? (Those are two different, equally important things.)

That depends. Knowing more about God *without* knowing God more makes us vulnerable to pride. We might put our confidence in how many verses we can quote, our clean lifestyle, or our spiritual gifts — rather than putting our confidence in Christ. Such pride is dangerous. *"God is opposed to the proud, but gives grace to the humble."* (James 4:6, NASB1995) Being in opposition to God is never a good thing.

When we seek to understand God's heart, in conjunction with our growing knowledge of Him, we are less vulnerable to pride but still unstable. And that's okay! The leaves — bowed face downward in subjection to the wind — are a picture of who we are when we draw near to God. The closer we get, the more we see our weaknesses and shortcomings and the more He humbles us.

This is exactly where we'll find the best of God's blessings. In Matthew 23:12, Jesus said,

And whoever exalts himself will be humbled,
and he who humbles himself will be exalted.

DAY 1 | PRAY:

Good and upright are you, Lord. Instruct me in your ways. Teach me humility, guide me in justice, and teach me. Guard my life and rescue me. (Psalm 25)

DAY 2 | MEMORIZE:

1 Peter 5:6

Therefore, humble yourselves under the mighty hand of God, that He may exalt you in due time.

DAY 3 | READ AND RESPOND:

Daniel 4:28-37

What was King Nebuchadnezzar prideful about?

Why did God take exception to Nebuchadnezzar's viewpoint about his kingdom?

How did God humble this Babylonian king?

What did Nebuchadnezzar conclude about God in Daniel 4:37?

DAY 4 | DO:

Press a leaf between the pages of a sturdy book. Even when it's dried, you will be able to tell the two sides apart. Keep it as a reminder to, as Micah said, "walk humbly with your God."

REFLECTIONS

DAY 5 | JOURNAL:

Record prayers, thoughts, or insights from your time with God.

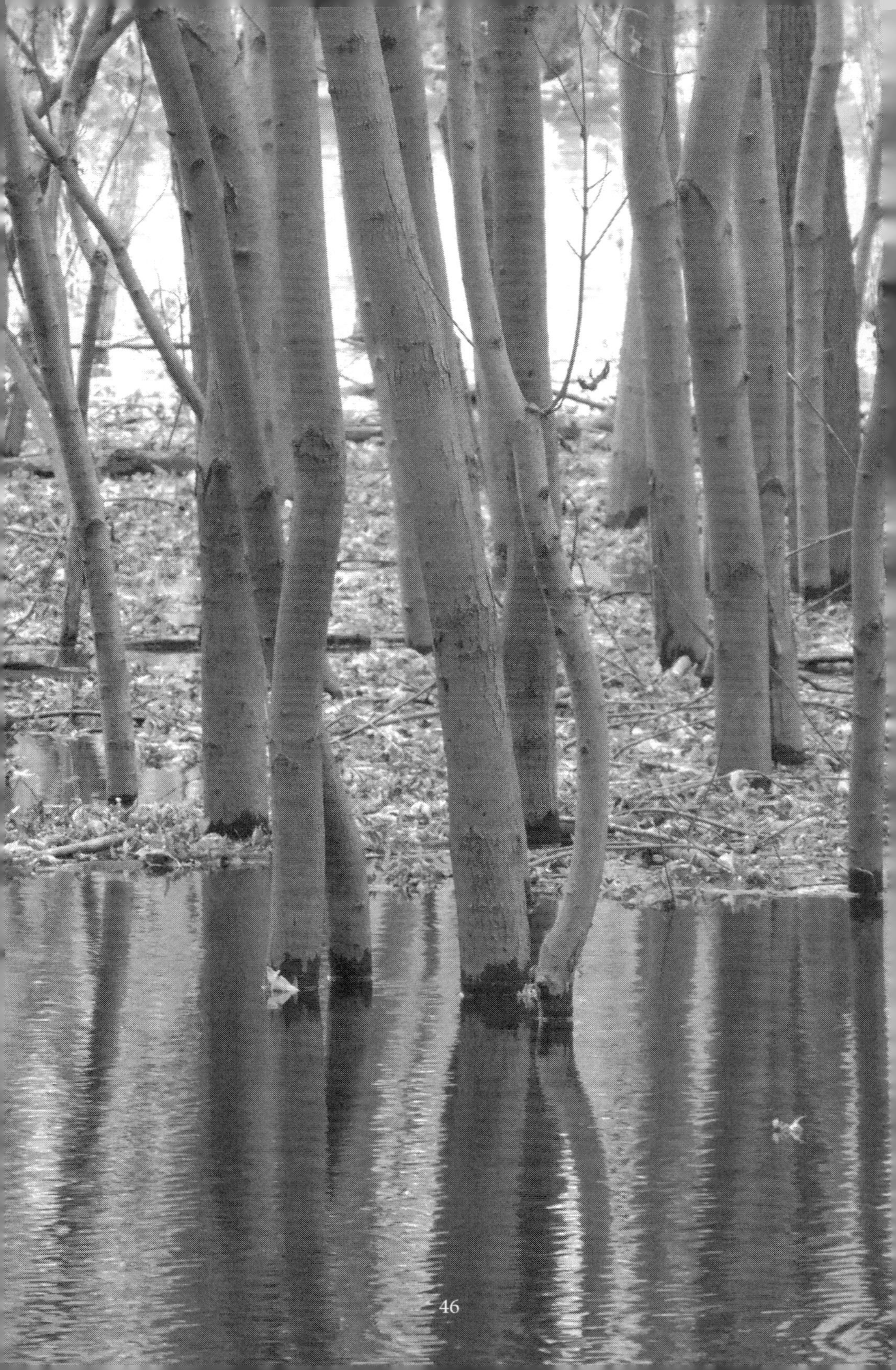

WEEK 12: FROM TESTING TO STANDING

CONSIDER:

I once found a striking stand of gray-barked trees growing in the backwaters of the mighty Mississippi River. Though they were knee-deep in water and muck, they looked healthy. Their bark was unscarred, their branches were fungus-free, and they stood straight and tall.

Despite being burdened with heavy snows and icy coats in the winter and battered by merciless winds during summer storms, among other threats, they remained standing.

By now, some have probably fallen, broken by harsh forces. They may break with the howling jeers of the cruel wind in their ears, or crumple under the weight of their load. But no doubt, many are still standing. A little beat up, perhaps — some twigs missing here, a fresh scar in the bark there — but still standing straight and tall. Steadfast. Immovable.

We go through seasons when we feel like we're standing knee-deep in mucky waters. We're battered by our fleshly desires, wounded by the sinful tendencies of others, and attacked by the forces of evil. Through God's living word, the Holy Spirit reminds us to expect tests and trials. We will face difficulties in this life.

Beloved, do not be surprised at the fiery ordeal among you, which comes upon you for your testing, as though some strange thing were happening to you.
(1 Peter 4:12, NASB1995)

Praise God, we don't have to break under our burdens. If we are steadfast and immovable, we are securely rooted in the truths of God's Word, living them out by God's power, day by day.

Every word of God proves true; He is a shield to those who take refuge in Him.
(Proverbs 30:5-6, ESV)

We do this best when we grow in close proximity — encouraging and exhorting one another, loving and instructing one another, serving and showing God's mercy to one another, praying for one another, and reminding one another of our ultimate hope in Christ.

God is faithful. He never changes. His Word is always true. We can firmly plant our feet in faith, knowing God will never fail us. He will give us the strength for the tasks He assigns us, so we can *"be strong in the Lord and in the strength of His might."* (Ephesians 6:10)

DAY 1 | PRAY:

Preserve me, O God, for I put my trust in you. You are my Lord. My goodness is nothing apart from you. I have set you always before me, Lord. Because you are at my right hand, I will not be moved. (Psalm 16)

DAY 2 | MEMORIZE:

1 Corinthians 15:58

Therefore, my beloved brethren, be steadfast, immovable, always abounding in the work of the Lord, knowing that your labor is not in vain in the Lord.

DAY 3 | READ AND RESPOND:

Genesis 22:1-19

What difficult thing did God ask Abraham to do as a test of his faith?
_____
_____
_____

Why did God test Abraham's faith? What did He want to know?
_____
_____
_____

What name for the Lord is introduced in this passage?
_____
_____
_____

What did God promise Abraham because his faith stood the test?
_____
_____
_____

DAY 4 | DO:

Find an uprooted tree in your area. What do you observe about the root system? Were the roots deep and clustered or shallow and spread out? What does this teach us about being rooted in God's Word?

REFLECTIONS

DAY 5 | JOURNAL:

Record prayers, thoughts, or insights from your time with God.

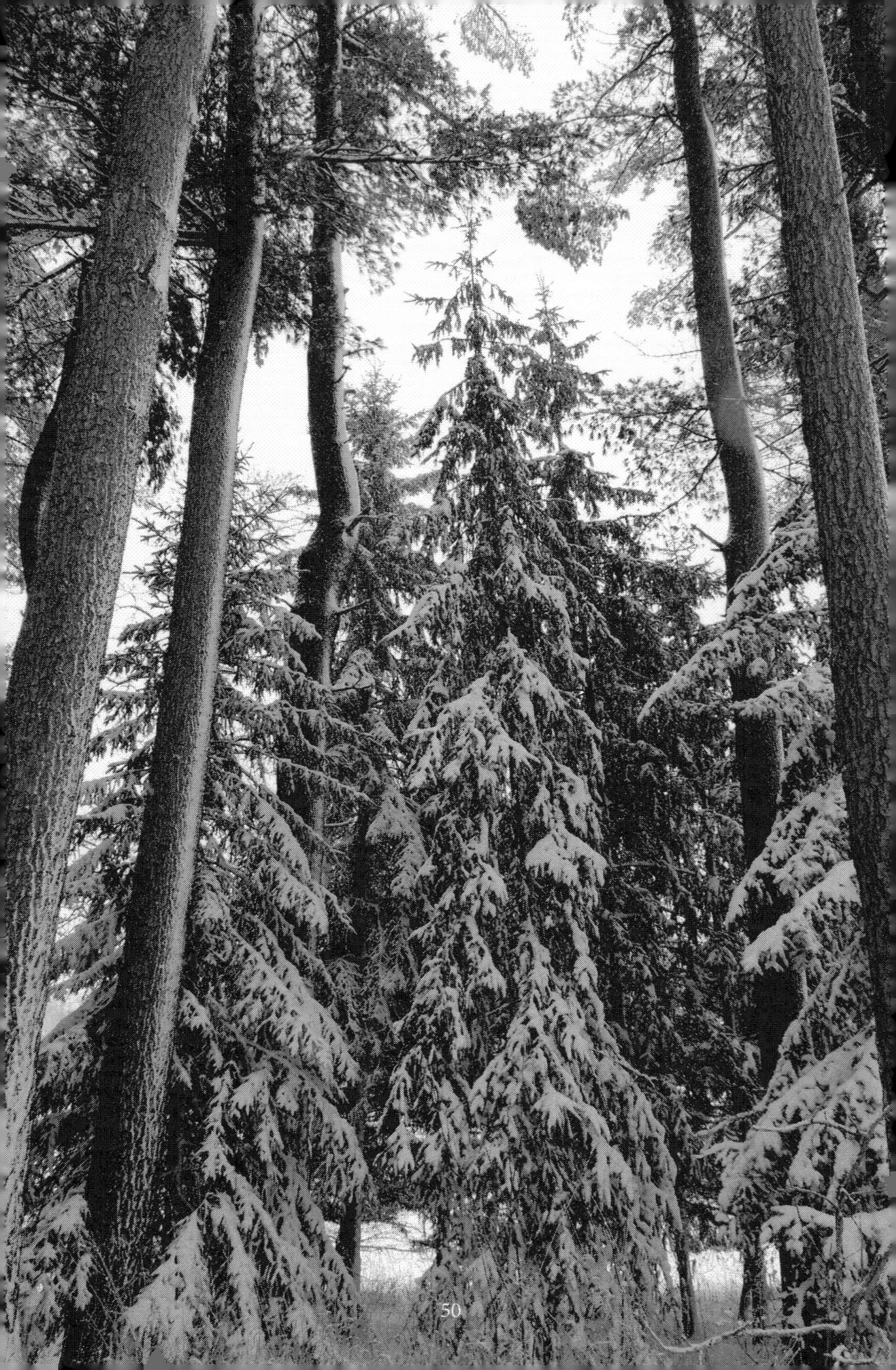

WEEK 13: FROM NOISE TO STILLNESS

CONSIDER:

Everything makes noise: vehicles, appliances, tools, computers, televisions, radios, phones. When people are outdoors, they often have earbuds stuck in their ears with amplified noise. Even churches, Christian concerts, and Christian camps have become noisy places, embracing the "loud is good" philosophy. It's almost an addiction.

Noisy really isn't God's modus operandi. Not that God never does loud. Thunder, hurricanes, tornadoes, wildfires, falling trees … all loud. They also seem to have a common thread. All are demonstrations of God's great might, and sometimes His wrath and judgment. But most of His day-to-day words — words of love, encouragement, reassurance, conviction, hope, and peace — are gentle and soft-spoken. God does not usually yell over the noise to get His child's attention.

God's voice is more like a snowy winter day, when chunky clusters of flakes tumble earthward, holding hands and dancing to a muted tune only they can hear. The snow muffles all the unwanted sounds. It's so quiet, profound stillness envelops the landscape. The whole world waits in silent homage to hear God whisper to His children, *"Be still, and know that I am God."* (Psalm 46:10)

"Be still, like a calm, winter day. Welcome silence into your life. Talk less. Turn off the unnecessary noises inside your head. Meditate on My word more. Turn off the external noises whenever possible. Be still so you can hear Me. Be still so you can know Me."

If we would hear God, we must be like the wind and the waves on the Sea of Galilee. Jesus *"got up and rebuked the wind and said to the sea, 'Hush, be still.' And the wind died down and it became perfectly calm."* (Mark 4:39, NASB1995)

Countless things scream for our attention every day. We can't just ignore their demanding volume, nor should we. Our daily responsibilities shouldn't be neglected. But if we can carve out a little daily time to listen to the whispering voice of our Maker, we will find solace in a stillness so deep it penetrates the soul like a calm, winter day. If we can spend some time reading the Bible and listening for the voice of the Spirit each day, we will come to know our God more fully.

DAY 1 | PRAY:

You alone are my rock and my salvation, God. You are my defense; I will not be shaken. My soul waits silently for you alone, for my expectation is from you. I will trust in you at all times. (Psalm 62)

DAY 2 | MEMORIZE:

Psalm 62:1

Truly my soul silently waits for God;
From Him comes my salvation.

DAY 3 | READ AND RESPOND:

1 Kings 19:1-18

In 1 Kings 18, Elijah had two great spiritual victories by God's mighty power. Why was he hiding in the wilderness?

_____
_____
_____

What was God's response to Elijah's pity party (verses 1-10)?

_____
_____

In verses 11-13, Elijah obeyed God and went and stood on the mountain. The Lord passed by him. What three things happened before God spoke to Elijah in a still, small voice?

_____
_____
_____

Why was Elijah discouraged? How can this passage reassure us when we are in similar circumstances?

_____
_____
_____

DAY 4 | DO:

Find a quiet place in your house, your yard, or perhaps a nearby park — preferably someplace you can visit easily and regularly. Leave your phone, music, and other distractions behind. Sit quietly for 10 to 15 minutes and listen for God's still, small voice.

REFLECTIONS

DAY 5 | JOURNAL:

Record prayers, thoughts, or insights from your time with God.

WEEK 14: FROM SEEKING TO DISCOVERING

CONSIDER:

I love a good storm.

Several years ago, I sat in our tire swing, which hangs from the muscular arm of an old oak, and watched a bank of storm clouds roll in. In the distance, thunder rumbled low and long. An uncanny flood of joy washed over me, as though the thunder had broken winter's fetters. I closed my eyes and faced the wind, fresh and warm with the scent of spring. I stretched out my arms, like I did when I was little, with a wish the wind could lift me from the ground and carry me above the trees.

The rain was slow and gentle at first, but it picked up power when a lightning bolt was followed almost instantly by a crash so loud the sound waves reverberated through me. I stayed a little longer, letting the rain wash away my cares.

I read a remarkable story about John Muir when I was in college. He loved a good storm, too. He once climbed to the tippy top of a Douglas fir, high in the Sierra Nevada mountains, and rode out a thunderstorm clinging to the tree trunk. I went inside when I considered what his demise could have been — and what mine could be.

Hosea 6:3 has these encouraging instructions for us:

So let us know, let us press on to know the Lord.
His going forth is as certain as the dawn.
And He will come to us like the rain,
like the spring rain watering the earth.
(NASB1995)

We can expend a great deal of energy pursuing uncertain things: comfort, happiness, security, respect, possessions — just to name a few. God instead urges us to pursue Him, the only sure thing.

If we seek Him, God promises to reveal Himself as certainly as the sun rises each morning. And as the sun's brightness and intensity increase throughout the day, God unveils Himself in ever greater ways. He promises to come like a spring rain, washing away our impurities, bringing life-giving refreshment, nourishing seeds of growth, and drenching us with blessings. Can the world offer a better promise than this?

DAY 1 | PRAY:

Those who keep your testimonies, who seek you with their whole hearts, are blessed. With my whole heart I seek you. Do not let me wander from your commandments! (Psalm 119)

DAY 2 | MEMORIZE:

Jeremiah 29:13

And you will seek Me and find Me when you search for Me with all your heart.

DAY 3 | READ AND RESPOND:

Deuteronomy 4:25-31

What did God warn the Israelites He would do if they began worshipping idols and pursuing other evil things?

_____
_____
_____

What does He promise will happen if they seek God instead?

_____
_____
_____

In verse 31, why will God be merciful if they turn back from their sin and obey Him? What will He remember?

_____
_____
_____

How is this passage applicable to us?

_____
_____
_____
_____

DAY 4 | DO:

Find a small fabric scrap and a washable marker — any color but red (which is not as washable as they claim). Is there something in your life you've allowed to usurp God's lordship? Write it on the fabric. When you're ready to let go of it, have a talk with God. Now, wash out the fabric. When it's dry, write a word on the fabric, in permanent marker, as a reminder of your desire to seek God wholeheartedly.

REFLECTIONS

DAY 5 | JOURNAL:

Record prayers, thoughts, or insights from your time with God.

(Photo credit: © Андрей KJ / Adobe Stock)

WEEK 15: FROM WANDERING TO FOLLOWING

CONSIDER:

We were nearly home when we saw a car parked on the roadside with its flashers on. We stopped to see if the driver needed help. "No, I'm fine. Just watch out for the herd ahead," she said. Beef cattle wandered down the middle of the road around the next bend. Even in Hicksville, USA, this is an unusual sight. Black angus, on a dark night, on an unlit blacktop road — we were thankful for the warning.

At first, my husband trailed slowly behind them, hesitant to pass. They began running, and we had a cattle drive underway. Yeehaw! Just substitute horsepower for horses and lose the long horns. Our concern was whether we were driving them toward or away from home. We decided it would be prudent to pass in the other lane.

Those beef cattle must have broken through their fence and wandered off. They were probably frightened by the unfamiliar highway sights and sounds. And without the farmer's familiar voice to guide them, they were "udderly" lost. (Sorry, I couldn't resist!)

We're compared to sheep in scripture, but cattle can go astray and turn their own way, just like people. (Isaiah 53:6) The outcome is the same. Consider all the people wandering aimlessly through life, lost and unsure which way to go. The voices they listen to are like our car driving the cattle who-knows-where — the blind leading the blind.

As Christ-followers, we know the comfort of a familiar, trustworthy voice. We are confident in God's guidance through life's twists and turns. The Bible is a lamp to our feet and a light to our path. (Psalm 119:105) We know our ultimate destination is heaven, so we never have to wander aimlessly.

We follow the only One who can bring light to the darkness that lies ahead. When Christ walked the earth, He had great compassion for the lost. He wept over Jerusalem, wishing He could gather them in His arms like a hen gathers her chicks under her wings. (Matthew 23:37) God entrusted us with His light so we can help those who are wandering fall in step with the only leader worth following.

You are the light of the world. A city that is set on a hill cannot be hidden ... Let your light so shine before men, that they may see your good works and glorify your Father in heaven. (Matthew 5:14,16)

DAY 1 | PRAY:

Let your light in me shine before men, so they may see my good works and glorify you, Father. I want my light to shine and give light to everyone around me. (Matthew 5)

DAY 2 | MEMORIZE:

John 8:12

Then Jesus spoke to them again, saying, "I am the light of the world. He who follows Me shall not walk in darkness, but have the light of life."

DAY 3 | READ AND RESPOND:

John 6:60-69

In verse 63, what does Jesus say about His words? What does this mean?

_____
_____

**Who initiates our relationship with God?
What statement in this passage supports this?**

_____
_____
_____

To find out why many of Christ's disciples walked away (verse 66), you have to go back and read verses 43-62. What reason did Peter give for not turning back?

_____
_____

Have you ever considered turning back? Why did you decide to continue following Jesus?

_____
_____
_____

DAY 4 | DO:

Make a list of people you follow on social media or in the news. What do you gain from following them? What do you gain from following Christ?

REFLECTIONS

DAY 5 | JOURNAL:

Record prayers, thoughts, or insights from your time with God.

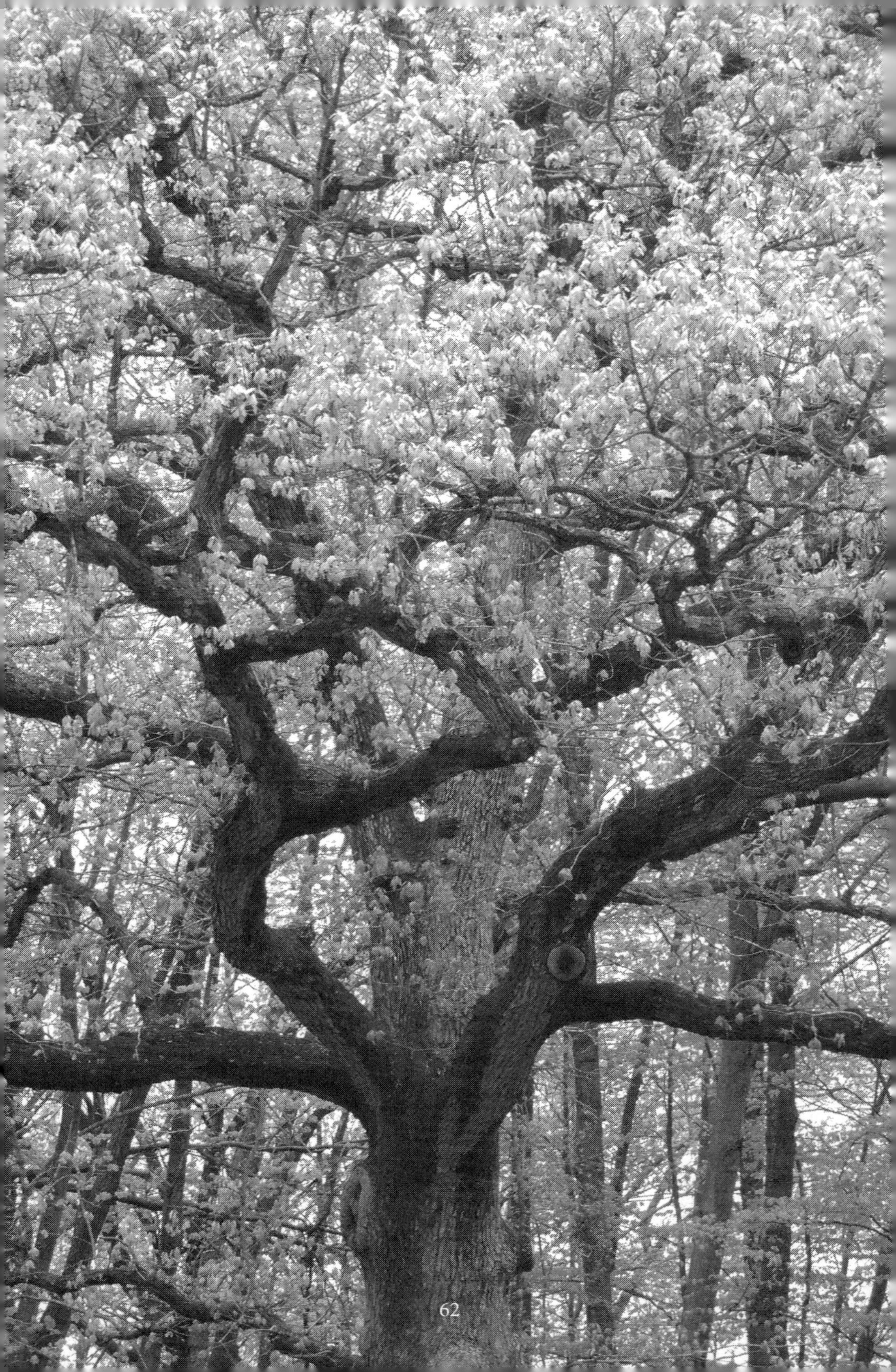

WEEK 16: FROM FLAWED TO PERFECTED

CONSIDER:

There's an oak tree down the road with an impressive burl on its trunk. If it were crafted into a bowl, it would hold a good five pounds of spaghetti smothered with meatballs and marinara.

Scientists don't know exactly why burls form, but they know stress is the trigger. The tree is attacked by insects, disease, or parasitic plants. To stop the invasion, it builds a defensive wall. Each year the tree sends more tissue to its vulnerable point, the burl grows. The tree is perfectly healthy, just flawed.

That imperfection will be with the tree throughout its life. The only way to harvest a burl, without damaging it, is to cut down the whole tree. The unique wood grain it forms often extends into the tree's trunk. Lopping it off would leave the tree vulnerable to disease and infestation and would ruin the burl.

Have you ever seen woodwork crafted from burls? The grain swirls and twists in bands of contrasting color. An artist with a good eye will make the burl into something that accentuates its beauty.

In 2 Corinthians 12:7b-9a, the apostle Paul said,

A thorn in the flesh was given to me, a messenger of Satan to buffet me, lest I be exalted above measure. Concerning this thing I pleaded with the Lord three times that it might depart from me. And He said to me, "My grace is sufficient for you, for My strength is made perfect in weakness."

Paul was flawed. He carried a burl with him his whole life. When he prayed for deliverance, rather than remove the threat, God infused His strength into Paul's most vulnerable spot. His imperfection became a demonstration of God's perfection. God took Paul's burl and crafted it into a one-of-a-kind masterpiece.

We all have burls we carry throughout our lives. Our imperfections take nothing from our usefulness in God's greater plans. It is in our vulnerable places that God demonstrates His perfect strength. We can be confident He will craft our lives into a one-of-a-kind masterpiece.

One day, we will join Paul in his perfected state. Until then, God strengthens us for the work He's assigned us. We'll fight physical battles against disease and weaknesses. We'll wage spiritual war against Satan and his minions. But in all things, God will be our shield and defender, our rock and our fortress, and our ever-present help in times of trouble.

DAY 1 | PRAY:

Lord, though I walk through troubles, you will revive me. You will stretch out your hand and save me. You, Lord, will perfect what concerns me. Your mercy, O Lord, endures forever. Do not forsake the works of your hands. (Psalm 138)

DAY 2 | MEMORIZE:

Ephesians 2:10

For we are His workmanship, created in Christ Jesus for good works, which God prepared beforehand that we should walk in them.

DAY 3 | READ AND RESPOND:

Luke 16:19-31

What thorn in the flesh did Lazarus bear in his lifetime?

_____
_____
_____

In contrast, what was the rich man's thorn?

_____
_____
_____

Lazarus allowed God's strength to be perfected in him. The rich man did not. What was the outcome for each man?

_____
_____
_____

Why do you think Jesus gave us this story?

_____
_____
_____

DAY 4 | DO:

Search "burl bowl images" on your computer. Take time to look at the varied wood grains in the bowls. Think about what makes each unique. Think about what makes you unique.

REFLECTIONS

DAY 5 | JOURNAL:

Record prayers, thoughts, or insights from your time with God.

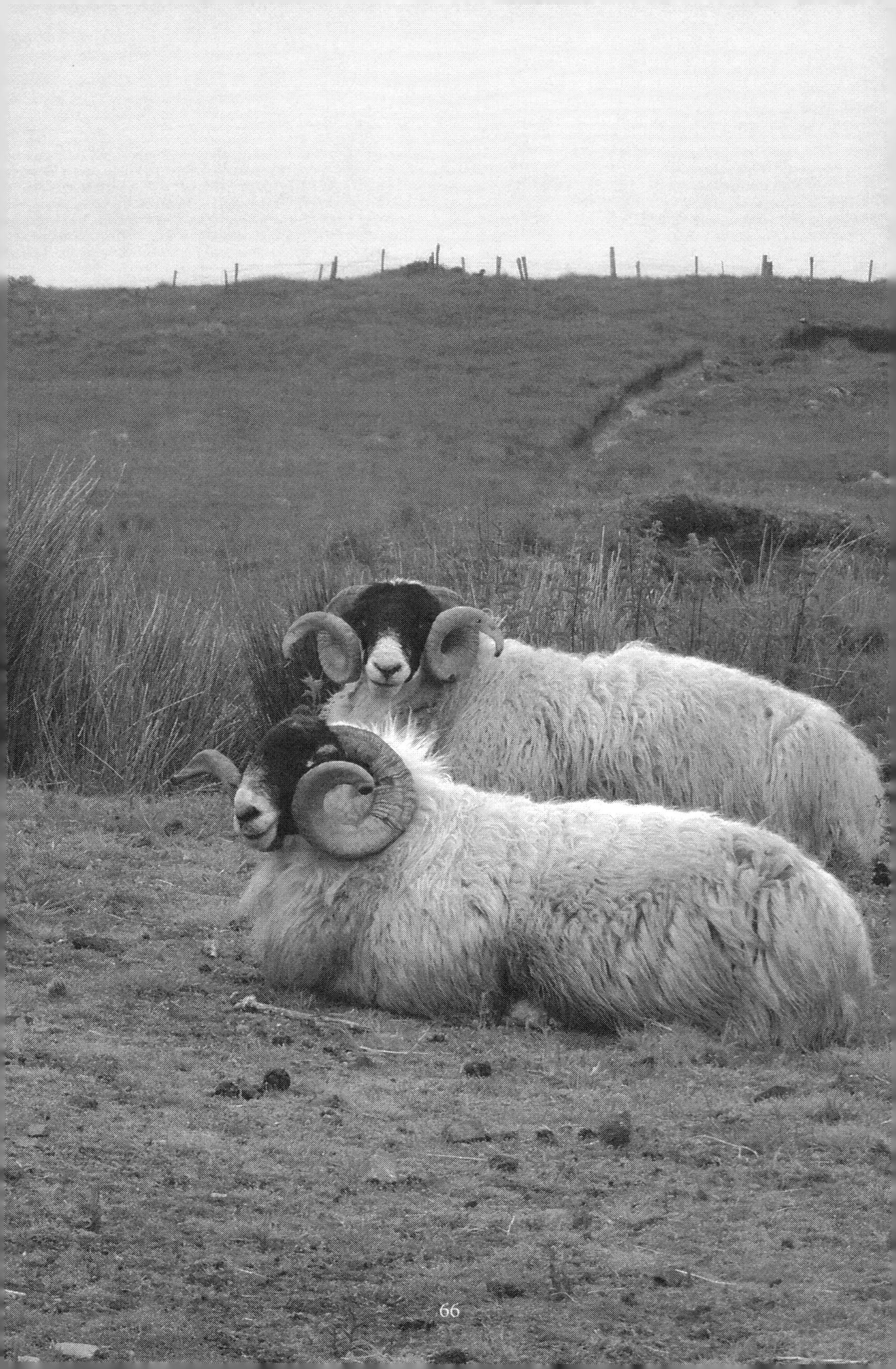

WEEK 17: FROM GOATS TO SHEEP

CONSIDER:

Our neighbor had a goat. He was essentially a lawnmower who kept the noxious weeds at bay. Goats can and will eat almost anything. He spent his days alone, munching away at whatever greenery he could find, then came home at night. He was friendly enough but had independent tendencies, as most goats do.

The trickiest part was keeping him confined. When I rode my bike past the remote land, I sometimes found him outside the fence. He had a knack for getting into mischief, though I suspect he was driven more by curiosity than naughtiness. It's amazing he survived some of the stunts he pulled!

Other than the fact they are both from the same animal family, sheep and goats have very little in common. Unlike goats, sheep are not opportunists when it comes to eating. They graze. The challenge for shepherds is the vast number of plants these woolly creatures find toxic. It takes diligence to keep them healthy.

Sheep are more timid than goats. They're comfortable just hanging out with the flock. They feel no need to express their independence by exploring places that capture their curiosity. That's not to say they never get themselves into trouble — they just aren't as adept at getting out of it as goats. Instead, they cry out for help, which is why they need a shepherd.

> *But when He saw the multitudes, He was moved with compassion for them, because they were weary and scattered, like sheep having no shepherd.* (Matthew 9:36)

The moral of this story is not that we should lack natural curiosity. While it's true our desire to understand the unknown can sometimes be dangerous, curious people have made revolutionary discoveries and uncovered still-unexplained wonders of God's creation.

The moral of the story is that we need a shepherd who will watch over us and rescue us when we are in trouble. We need Jesus, the Good Shepherd.

> *He will feed His flock like a shepherd;*
> *He will gather the lambs with His arm,*
> *And carry them in His bosom,*
> *And gently lead those who are with young.* (Isaiah 40:11)

We also need our flock. All the "one another" and "live in unity" commands in God's Word make it impossible to conclude we're meant to live out our faith in solitude. Rubbing shoulders with other sheep comforts, strengthens and encourages us. It also makes us less vulnerable to Satan, the crouching lion seeking to devour the weak and isolated sheep.

DAY 1 | PRAY:

Lord, I was like a sheep going astray, but I have now returned to the Shepherd and Overseer of my soul. You are my Shepherd, I will want for nothing. You restore my soul. You lead me in the paths of righteousness for your name's sake. (1 Peter 2, Psalm 23)

DAY 2 | MEMORIZE:

John 10:27-28

My sheep hear My voice, and I know them, and they follow Me. And I give them eternal life, and they shall never perish; neither shall anyone snatch them out of My hand.

DAY 3 | READ AND RESPOND:

Matthew 25:31-46

How does the scene Jesus described in this parable parallel with the scene in Revelation 20:12-15?

_____

_____

What did the sheep do that the goats did not do?

_____

_____

When talking about the kindnesses His sheep showed others, Jesus said, "Inasmuch as you did it to one of the least of these My brethren, you did it to Me." What does that mean? Why is that true?

_____

_____

Spiritually speaking, can goats become sheep? Based on John 3:16-18, what must we do to switch flocks?

_____

_____

DAY 4 | DO:

If you've never seen a shepherd call his sheep, take a few minutes to watch "The Good Shepherd & His Sheep" on YouTube.
You can find it at: *https://www.youtube.com/watch?v=Coq_grSFINs*

REFLECTIONS

DAY 5 | JOURNAL:

Record prayers, thoughts, or insights from your time with God.

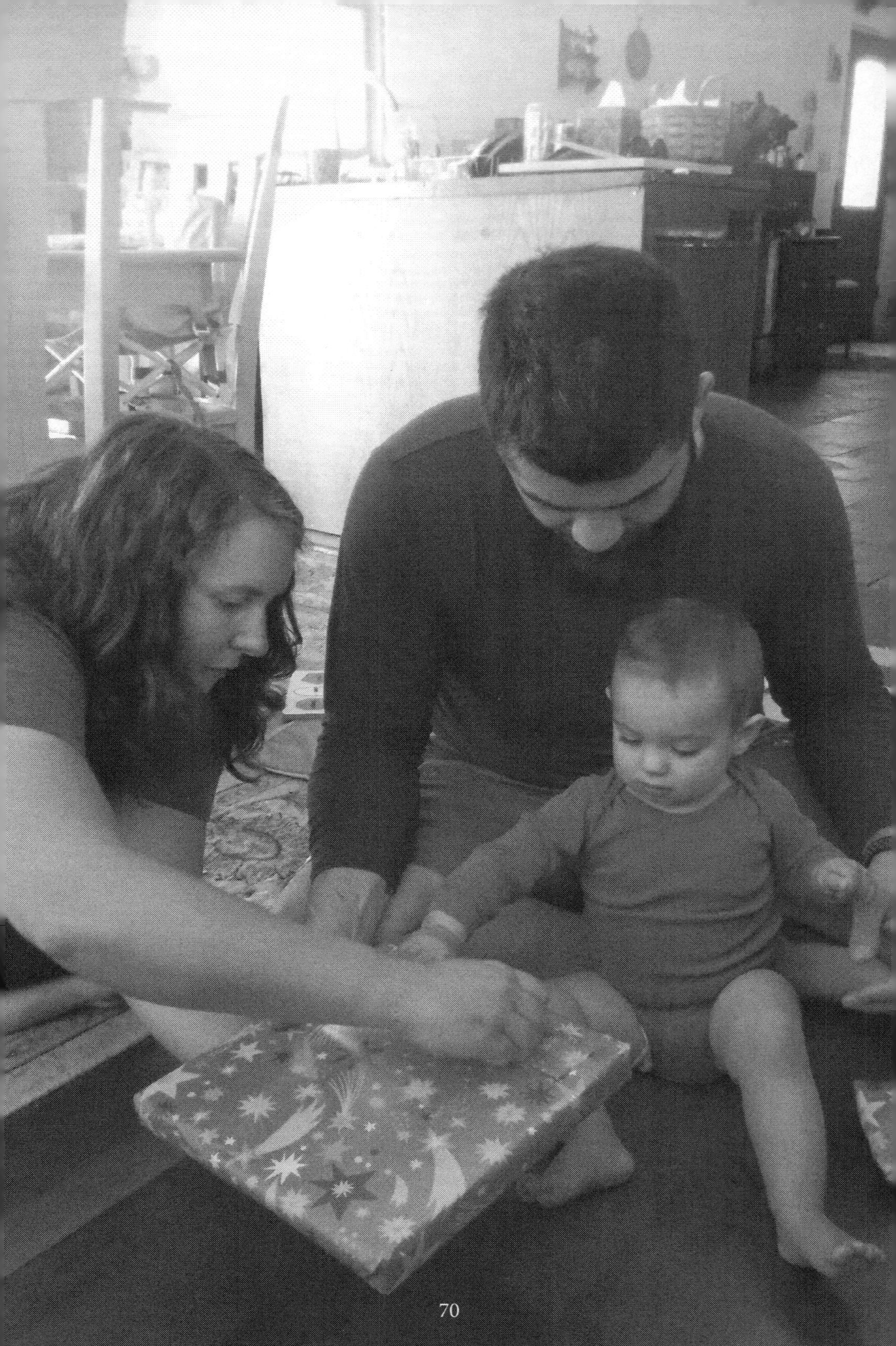

WEEK 18: FROM ORPHANS TO GOD'S CHILDREN

CONSIDER:

In ancient Rome, parents were encouraged to kill any baby with a deformity. In *On the Laws*, Cicero stated, "Deformed infants shall be killed." The "deformity" could be anything from an unwanted child or a child the father deemed was the wrong sex, to a sickly or physically imperfect child. The Stoic philosopher Seneca stated in his treatise, *On Anger*, "... unnatural progeny we destroy; we drown even children at birth who are weakly and abnormal."

The pagan Roman culture placed no value on human life, which left infants exposed and vulnerable. Some were taken in by families as slaves. Some were rescued as playmates for a family's natural children. Sadly, others were rescued for nothing more than prostitution.

One mark of the early church was their compassion for these abandoned children. In stark contrast to their culture, Christians believed — to the point of action — these children were created in God's image. They were worthy of dignity and care. Believers pulled drowning babies to safety. They scoured dung heaps for infants left to die from exposure. Often, they were only able to comfort these babies in their final moments and give them a respectable burial. But they raised the children who lived as their own.

Their actions reflected their relationship with God, an example the church continued to emulate by providing health care, education, and daily essentials for vulnerable people.

Even if we're born into loving, attentive families, we begin our lives outside of God's family. As Jesus said in John 8:44, *"You are of your father the devil, and the desires of your father you want to do."* But when we accept God's free gift of salvation, we are reborn. God rescues us from our spiritual demise and adopts us into His family.

> *But as many as received Him, to them He gave the right to become children of God, to those who believe in His name: who were born, not of blood, nor of the will of the flesh, nor of the will of man, but of God.* (John 1:12-13)

Then, God asks us to pay it forward. Do you remember what it was like to be orphaned, without a loving Father? When we recall the joy of being welcomed into a family, we are more prone to care for the practical needs of physically orphaned children and extend an invitation to the spiritually orphaned to make peace with God and join His family.

DAY 1 | PRAY:

Lord, you are a father of the fatherless, a defender of widows in your holy habitation. You establish those who are alone in families and lead out prisoners with singing. I sing praises to your name. (Psalm 68)

DAY 2 | MEMORIZE:

Romans 8:15-16

For you did not receive the spirit of bondage again to fear, but you received the Spirit of adoption by whom we cry out, "Abba, Father." The Spirit Himself bears witness with our spirit that we are children of God.

DAY 3 | READ AND RESPOND:

Galatians 4:1-7

What parallels does Paul draw between the child of an heir and a slave? What is he saying?

What are "the elements of the world" we were in bondage to before God adopted us?

Verse 6 is very similar to our memory verses for the week. Record a moment when you were very aware of the Spirit confirming that you are God's child.

Read John 15:15. How does this verse relate to Galatians 4:7?

DAY 4 | DO:

Ask God to show you ways you can care for the practical and spiritual needs of vulnerable people. Ministries serving widows, orphans, the homeless, and victims of human trafficking are often looking for prayer partners and volunteer workers, as well as financial donors.

REFLECTIONS

DAY 5 | JOURNAL:

Record prayers, thoughts, or insights from your time with God.

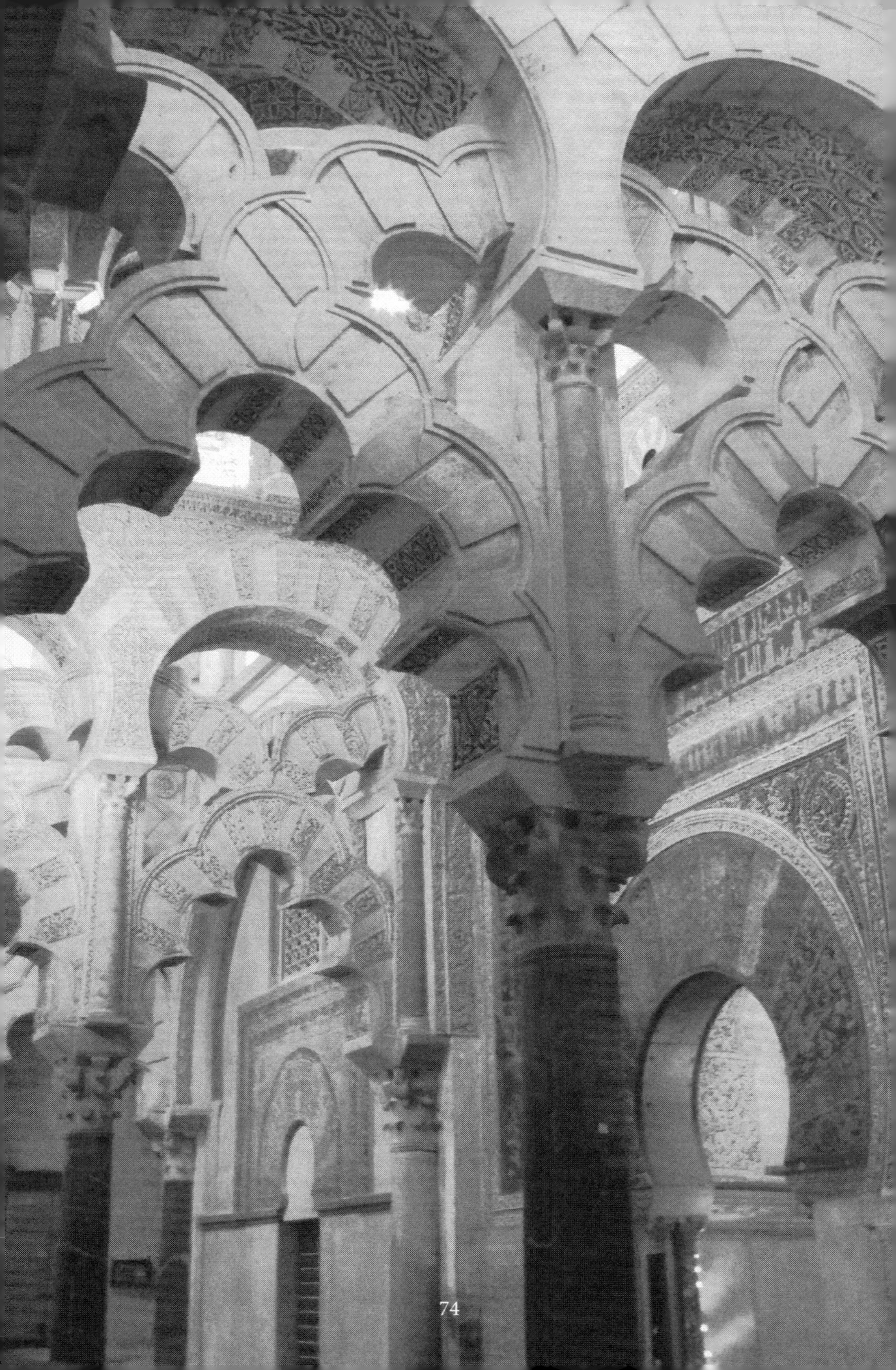

WEEK 19: FROM ALIENS TO CITIZENS

CONSIDER:

My husband and I visited Spain several years ago. We saw historic wonders, enjoyed mountain vistas, and watched sunsets from the beach. As much as we enjoyed taking in what the culture offered, we were strangers. We were visitors who struggled with the slower pace of life, misunderstood some of the customs, and bumbled what little Spanish we spoke. We were the only ones not wearing winter coats in the "cold" weather (72 degrees Fahrenheit).

Our alien status was accentuated when we got a parking ticket. We tried using our limited command of Spanish to ask a police officer what we should do. He looked at us like we were speaking Swahili. It took a translation app to settle the ordeal. At the end of the week, we returned home. Our stay was short-lived.

Once we are adopted into God's family, we have a new home address: 1 Mansion Lane, Heaven. Although our bodies remain earthbound, our time on earth is short. It's like a vacation in Spain. Our true home is heaven, and our hearts and souls now align with the eternal things of God.

> *Beloved, I beg you as sojourners and pilgrims, abstain from fleshly lusts which war against the soul.* (1 Peter 2:11)

We no longer pursue temporal things. We lay up treasures in heaven rather than on earth. We choose what glorifies God rather than what satisfies our flesh. The needs of others begin to outweigh our own. We speak a foreign language that points toward God. The citizens of Earth don't understand it. We can measure whether the spirit of truth is in others by whether they can hear — not just listen but hear — God's truths.

> *They are of the world. Therefore they speak as of the world, and the world hears them. We are of God. He who knows God hears us; he who is not of God does not hear us. By this we know the spirit of truth.* (1 John 4:5-6)

As sojourners on earth and citizens of heaven, we will sometimes feel as displaced as a stranger visiting from a foreign land. Just like immigrants to a new country seek out people from their own cultural background for support and encouragement, believers seek out each other for the same reasons. We walk side by side toward our heavenly home, inviting others to join our journey, until our time on earth is done.

DAY 1 | PRAY:

Thank you, Father, that I am no longer a stranger and foreigner, but a fellow citizen with the saints and members of the household of God. I now have a true heavenly home. Hallelujah! (Ephesians 2)

DAY 2 | MEMORIZE:

Philippians 3:20

For our citizenship is in heaven, from which we also eagerly wait for the Savior, the Lord Jesus Christ.

DAY 3 | READ AND RESPOND:

Hebrews 11:1-16

What are some of the unseen things we hope for as Christians?

_____
_____
_____

What were the promises the men and women of faith in verses 4-11 could see but did not receive?

_____
_____
_____

How did this make them realize they were strangers and pilgrims on earth?

_____
_____
_____

What is the better country they desired (and we desire)? Would you ever choose to go back to where you came from? Why or why not?

_____
_____
_____

DAY 4 | DO:

Draw a picture that demonstrates what it's like to feel out of place or like a stranger in a foreign land.

DAY 5 | JOURNAL:

Record prayers, thoughts, or insights from your time with God.

(Photo credit: © [EcoView] / Adobe Stock)

WEEK 20: FROM LONGING TO SATISFACTION

CONSIDER:

I grew up in the days before cable TV and streaming services. In our house, we had reliable signals for ABC and CBS. PBS and NBC were iffy. Way back then, the quasi-equivalent to Animal Planet was Mutual of Omaha's Wild Kingdom and occasional National Geographic prime time specials.

These shows were my first introduction to the local watering hole (no, that is not a reference to the neighborhood bar). Out there on the Serengeti, where the rains are seasonal and water is a rare commodity, all of the animals gather and drink from the same pool. It's a great setup for the predators. They can get a drink and nab a snack all in one stop.

It must be a bit nerve-racking for the potential prey, though. The gazelles, zebras, and wildebeests probably keep an eye on the lions, cheetahs, and hyenas. I don't think there's an animal code of honor that stops the watering hole from becoming the killing fields. Imagine how thirst-driven those vulnerable animals must be to risk their lives for a drink of water.

Perhaps it was a similar scene that inspired the sons of Korah to write this in Psalm 42:1-2:

As the deer pants for the water brooks,
So pants my soul for You, O God.

My soul thirsts for God, for the living God.
When shall I come and appear before God?

They compared their longing for God's presence to a deer panting with thirst as it searched for water — a life necessity. Being in God's presence wasn't a luxury or a desire to satisfy a short-lived craving. They were pursuing the source and sustainer of their lives with desperate fervor. When we have food on the table, gas in the tank, and a roof overhead, our flesh can get mighty comfortable with God's practical provisions. Though it's not in our nature to long for God, we can ask Him to create an urgent longing in our hearts and souls to dwell in His presence and find fullness of joy.

Our good Father wants to satisfy our souls with the bread of life. He wants to give us living water so we never thirst again. He wants to shelter us under His wings. He wants our desire for His presence to overpower our fear of surrendering our lives to His lordship, knowing this is the only place our souls will find satisfaction.

DAY 1 | PRAY:

I am blessed because you chose me and brought me near to live in your courts. Thank you, Lord. I will be satisfied with the goodness of your house, of your holy temple. You are my confidence! (Psalm 65)

DAY 2 | MEMORIZE:

Psalm 16:11

You will show me the path of life;
In Your presence is fullness of joy;
At Your right hand are pleasures forevermore.

DAY 3 | READ AND RESPOND:

Psalm 27

In verses 1-3, why did the psalmist have nothing to fear?

_____
_____
_____

In verses 4-6, what was the one thing the psalmist sought, and why?

_____
_____
_____

In verses 7-10, what was the psalmist's response to God?

_____
_____
_____

What instructions did the psalmist leave us in verse 14?

_____
_____
_____

DAY 4 | DO:

For at least one day, every time you take a drink of water, praise God for a way in which He has satisfied or is satisfying your spiritual thirst.

Write your praises down.

DAY 5 | JOURNAL:

Record prayers, thoughts, or insights from your time with God.

(Photo credit: © [DC Studio] / Adobe Stock)

WEEK 21: FROM WAITING TO FULFILLMENT

CONSIDER:

It was a pretty typical waiting room, in most respects. The walls, however, lacked the nondescript "art" intended to calm the wait-ees. Instead, four large, toothy muskies hung on the walls. Toothy seemed consistent with a dental office. And stuffed fish? Well, that's Wisconsin. The men want to display their "trophies" and most of their wives don't want "dead stuff" in the house — which is probably how the stuffed fish ended up at the office.

I passed the time somewhat restlessly, waiting to the serenade of high-pitched drills and airy suction tubes. I don't mind going to the dentist. The waiting, however, I could live without.

God puts us in His spiritual waiting room from time to time. Between appointments, He nurtures us and prepares us for what lies ahead. Sometimes we get impatient, eager to move on. It's hard to say, as David did, *"I waited patiently for the Lord"* (Psalm 40:1a), but in God's perfect time, He gives us clear direction. Then we can say with certainty, *"He inclined to me, and heard my cry."* (Psalm 40:1b)

Our whole earthly journey is one big waiting room. Each day is preparation for that final day when all God purposed will be fulfilled. Imperfection will fade away in the glory of God's perfection.

1 Corinthians 13:12 says,

"For now we see in a mirror dimly..."

Fog clouds our vision of heavenly things. We try, based on things revealed in scripture, to imagine what God has waiting for us in heaven. But daily duties, physical and emotional pain, enslavement to time, and concerns of this fallen world distort our view of the things to come.

"... but then face to face."

What a wonderful, fearful day it will be when we see Jesus.

DAY 1 | PRAY:

I remain confident of this, Lord. I will see your goodness in the land of the living. I will wait for you, Lord. I will be strong and take heart and wait for you. (Psalm 27)

DAY 2 | MEMORIZE:

Micah 7:7

Therefore I will look to the Lord;
I will wait for the God of my salvation;

My God will hear me.

DAY 3 | READ AND RESPOND:

Exodus 2:11-3:14

Why was Moses in Midian?

What was he doing while he was there?

What assignment did God give to Moses?

Moses was reluctant at first. What did God promise Moses, to give him the courage to obey?

DAY 4 | DO:

The next time you steam up the bathroom mirror, try to make out your reflection through the fog on the mirror and then wipe it away with a towel and look again. Make note of any thoughts you have in your journal.

REFLECTIONS

DAY 5 | JOURNAL:

Record prayers, thoughts, or insights from your time with God.

(Photo credit: [Eugeniusz Dudzinski] / Adobe Stock)

JOURNEYING WITH OTHERS (WEEKS 22-36)

"He loves me. He loves me not. He loves me. He loves me not." As a little girl, I would pluck the petals off a daisy, one by one, to see whether my latest crush felt the same way about me. I've outgrown dissecting daisies. I pick them for sheer enjoyment these days. They are fascinating flowers.

Each daisy is a combination of two flower types: ray and disc. The yellow center, or disc, is made up of hundreds of tiny individual flowers, each with its own reproductive system. The petals are ray flowers. All the parts together form one lovely, compound flower — arguably the most prevalent flower in the world. It grows on every continent except Antarctica.

The universal church, which thrives throughout the world, is one entity made up of many individuals — just like the daisy. The Bible has much to say about the "oneness" of all who put their hope in Christ. Consider Ephesians 4:4-6:

There is one body and one Spirit, just as you were called in one hope of your calling; one Lord, one faith, one baptism; one God and Father of all, who is above all, and through all, and in you all.

As we all know, church families are a little dysfunctional, much like our flesh-and-blood families. Okay, sometimes they're *a lot* dysfunctional. Bickering — and subsequent side-choosing — often surface. But the more we abide in Christ, the more spiritual fruit we'll bear — *"love, joy, peace, longsuffering, kindness, goodness, faithfulness, gentleness, self-control."* (Galatians 5:22-23) The more spiritual fruit we bear, the more functional we'll be. And the better we'll all get along. We can live harmoniously with one another, even when we don't see eye to eye. The goal is oneness, not sameness.

That's not to suggest we should pursue harmony at all costs. It's dangerous to sacrifice God's truths to achieve unity. While we can compromise when there's room to differ in personal convictions, compromising on core doctrines will only allow false teaching to undermine the church. Rupertus Meldenius summarized it best: "In essentials unity, in non-essentials liberty, in all things charity."

In Romans 12:18 Paul tells us, *"if it is possible"* and *"as much as depends on each of us,"* we should live at peace with others. By the way, that includes our parents, spouses, and children. Peace and unity aren't always possible, because we are broken, sinful people. Paul knew it. God knows it. We know it, too. But we can pray for the fruit of His Spirit to be outward evidence of our oneness in Christ until we are complete in Him.

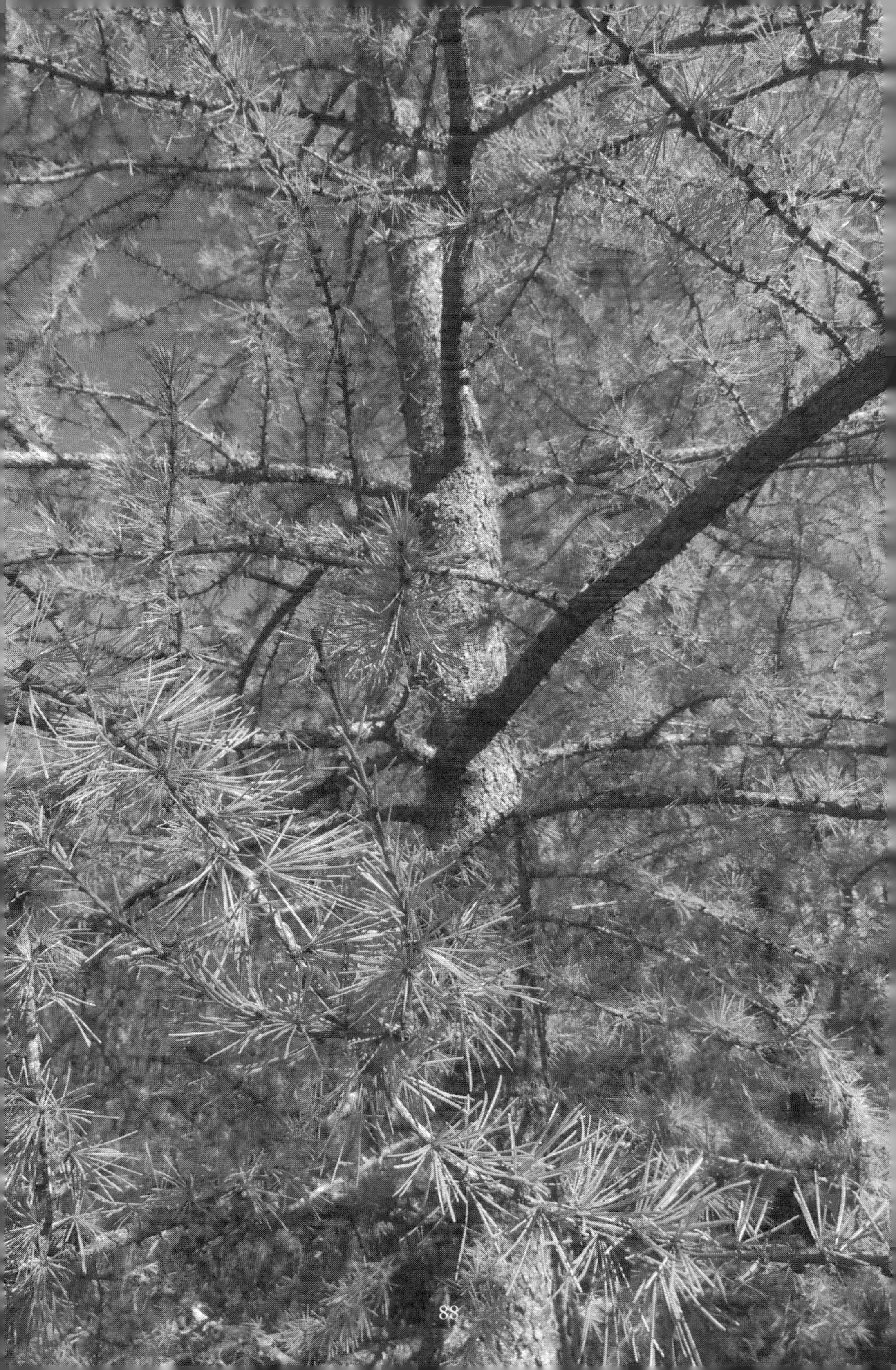

WEEK 22: FROM REJECTION TO ACCEPTANCE

CONSIDER:

I admire tamaracks for their quirky ways. They're the platypus of the plant kingdom. They challenge the norm. They refuse to conform, and in their nonconformity is a singular beauty. Each year, when other evergreens live up to their names, tamaracks take a countercultural stand. Unwilling to comply with societal constraints, they join ranks with the leaf-bearers. Their pale green needle pom-poms turn gold, the color they wear for several weeks before disrobing. They alone, among the evergreens, face winter's fury without their fur coats.

In our secular world, clinging to the cross is countercultural. We're like tamaracks in an evergreen world. It gets pretty cold out there! What we hold dear is attacked in the media, in our schools, and in the marketplace. We stand apart — shamed, scorned, and villainized. The culture wants everyone dressed in the same green coat year-round. There is no place, in that world, for the soul of a different color.

When we are born into God's family, we face both rejection and acceptance. The world, including some friends and family members, rejects us and all we represent. Paul instructs us to approach these people with kindness and sensitivity so we might win them over to Christ.

> *Walk in wisdom toward those who are outside, redeeming the time. Let your speech always be with grace, seasoned with salt, that you may know how you ought to answer each one.* (Colossians 4:5-6)

When our tight friendship with the world ends, we've put worldly things behind us. That's good! Compared to the life-or-death price many Christians pay for their faith, it's a small sacrifice. But rejection still leaves us wounded. Thankfully, our Great Physician *"heals the brokenhearted and binds up their wounds."* (Psalm 147:3)

We can find comfort in our Father's acceptance. New friends and a like-minded family welcome us. We have an eternal home, a place to lay up indestructible treasures. We're now on friendly terms with God, under the umbrella of His unconditional acceptance.

> *Now may the God of patience and comfort grant you to be like-minded toward one another, according to Christ Jesus, that you may with one mind and one mouth glorify the God and Father of our Lord Jesus Christ. Therefore receive one another, just as Christ also received us, to the glory of God.* (Romans 15:5-7)

DAY 1 | PRAY:

Your divine power, Father, has given me all things pertaining to life and godliness, through my knowledge of you. You have given me great and precious promises, through which I may take part in your divine nature, having escaped the corruption of this world. I praise you, Father! (2 Peter 1)

DAY 2 | MEMORIZE:

John 1:12

But as many as received Him, to them He gave the right to become children of God, to those who believe in His name.

DAY 3 | READ AND RESPOND:

John 15:18-27

Why will the world hate us if we follow Christ?
_____
_____
_____

Should we be surprised when we are rejected or persecuted? Why or why not?
_____
_____
_____

Why did the world hate Jesus? Why does He say this means they hated His Father also?
_____
_____
_____

How does the Holy Spirit help us?
_____
_____
_____

DAY 4 | DO:

Find a magnet. Most people have one hanging on the fridge somewhere. Find a metal paper clip and a penny. See which is attracted to the magnet. Consider why one is drawn to the magnet and the other isn't. Note any parallels you see to why people are or are not drawn to God.

REFLECTIONS

DAY 5 | JOURNAL:

Record prayers, thoughts, or insights from your time with God.

(Photo credit: © [lmphilip] / Adobe Stock)

JOURNEYING WITH OTHERS

WEEK 23: FROM STRANGERS TO FAMILY

CONSIDER:

In her book *Unlikely Friendships*, Jennifer Holland tells the story of a 600-pound "baby" hippopotamus (Owen) and a 130-year-old giant tortoise (Mzee). After a tsunami struck Kenya in 2004, Owen and Mzee found themselves in the same wildlife sanctuary. They formed an unexpected bond.

It began when Owen crouched behind Mzee as if hiding behind a boulder. Each time Mzee got annoyed and moved, Owen followed. By morning, they were cuddling as best a hippo and giant tortoise could. Workers at the rescue facility theorized the young hippo was missing its bloat (group of hippos) and was looking for companionship.

While Mzee was reluctant at first — tortoises aren't known for their warm, snuggly personalities — the gentle giant not only gave in but became Owen's role model. Owen ate what Mzee ate and picked up other non-hippo habits. They even began communicating with their own language of low rumbling sounds. Two strangers became their own small family.

Ephesians 2:19 says,

> *"Now, therefore, you are no longer strangers and foreigners, but fellow citizens with the saints and members of the household of God."*

Until we begin following Christ, God is a stranger to us. We might think we know who God is. We might think we understand His house rules. After all, we've heard what others say about Him and His expectations. But we're still standing at the gate, staring over the picket fence, wondering what it's like to call God "Abba, Father" and belong to His family.

Once we're insiders, fellow citizens of God's household, everything changes. Instead of knowing about God, we begin knowing God. Instead of getting directions into unfamiliar territory from fellow foreigners, we consult God's Word and our new family for guidance.

Although the members of God's family can be as different from one another as Owen and Mzee, we develop strong ties with the Holy Spirit. New adoptees follow the lead of those who are older, heeding Paul's instructions in 1 Corinthians 11:1: *"Imitate me, just as I also imitate Christ."* We seek out mutual encouragement and companionship because we are spiritually like-minded, despite our varied life experiences, personalities, and gifts.

These friendships go beyond anything this world offers, because Christ is in us. Through God's sovereign presence in us, we are eternally united to those who walk beside us, those who went before us, and those who will come after us.

DAY 1 | PRAY:

Father, as I have opportunity, let me do good to all, especially to those who are part of the household of faith. Do not let me grow weary of doing good. (Galatians 6)

DAY 2 | MEMORIZE:

Hebrews 13:15-16

Therefore by Him let us continually offer the sacrifice of praise to God, that is, the fruit of our lips, giving thanks to His name. But do not forget to do good and to share, for with such sacrifices God is well pleased.

DAY 3 | READ AND RESPOND:

Ecclesiastes 4:9-12

This passage is often read at weddings. Besides brides and grooms, who can gain something from the lesson in this passage?

_____
_____
_____

What reasons does Solomon offer for his *"two are better than one"* statement?

_____
_____
_____

Have you been in a situation where you found this to be true?

_____
_____
_____

Why is the bond between two strands even stronger with a third strand?

_____
_____
_____

DAY 4 | DO:

Find three strands of string, rope, yarn, or floss. Braid them together. Clearly, the braided strands will be harder to cut or break than the individual strands. Do you notice any other differences between the braided and unbraided strands?

REFLECTIONS

DAY 5 | JOURNAL:

Record prayers, thoughts, or insights from your time with God.

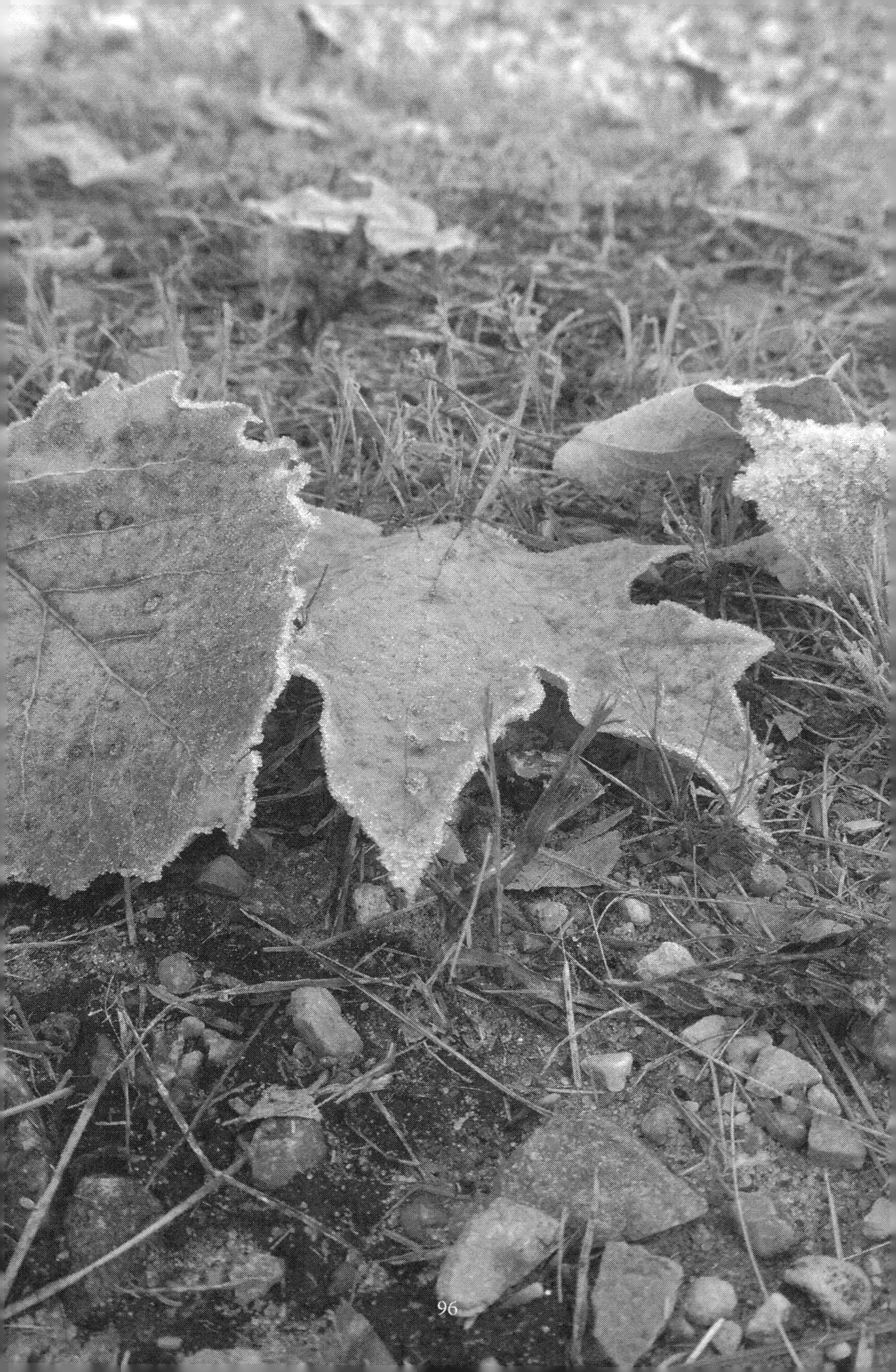

WEEK 24: FROM ISOLATION TO FELLOWSHIP

CONSIDER:

Every autumn, spent leaves fall and flit away on the breeze. No longer anchored to their respective trees, they whirl wistfully below a steel blue sky threatening to pour out its soggy contents. Eventually they land. Unless their footing is firm, however, they'll tumble along with passing winds until something pins them down.

The leaf showers always bring Ephesians 4:14-15 to mind. Paul said we're equipped with unique spiritual gifts to glorify God and spur one another on to maturity. Then he said,

> *As a result, we are no longer to be children, tossed here and there by waves and carried about by every wind of doctrine, by the trickery of men, by craftiness in deceitful scheming; but speaking the truth in love, we are to grow up in all aspects into Him who is the head, even Christ.* (NASB1995)

Spiritual maturity doesn't happen overnight. We can't anticipate it and it tends to come in sometimes-painful spurts, just like physical growth. If we aren't careful, our growth can be stunted by improper nurturing.

God gave us His written word to speak His truths. He gives us the Holy Spirit to lead us in His truths. And He gives us each other to spur us on in His truths. The commands to love, encourage, serve, be kind to, and rebuke one another are impossible to obey in a vacuum. Whose burdens will we bear? Whose interests will we put before our own? Who will we encourage if we aren't together? And, conversely, who will bear our burdens, prioritize our needs, and encourage us?

> *As iron sharpens iron, so a man sharpens the countenance of his friend.*
> (Proverbs 27:17)

Granted, togetherness can get messy. We will hurt and offend each other (ergo the "forgive one another" thing). Let's be honest. Sometimes, our nasty little selves would rather shove someone off the trail than help them along it. By the power of the Spirit, we can lend others a helping hand as we bumble forward together.

When we neglect God's Word, ignore the Holy Spirit's promptings, and isolate ourselves, we lose our anchor. We're like fall leaves riding the wind, rolling restlessly along until something pins us down. We're vulnerable to false doctrines, susceptible to Satan's lies, and in danger of being spiritually stunted. Maturing spiritually begins at our birth into Christ's family and ends when we stand before our Lord, complete in Christ!

DAY 1 | PRAY:

Let me go up to your house with your people, O Lord. You will teach us your ways and we will walk in your paths. Let us walk in your light, O Lord. (Isaiah 2)

DAY 2 | MEMORIZE:

Matthew 18:20

For where two or three are gathered together in My name, I am there in the midst of them.

DAY 3 | READ AND RESPOND:

Hebrews 10:19-25

Why can we boldly come before God's throne, individually and corporately?
_____
_____
_____
_____

What is the "confession of our hope" we can cling to?
_____
_____
_____

What is it we are not supposed to forsake or neglect?
_____
_____
_____

What reasons does this passage give for gathering together?
_____
_____
_____

DAY 4 | DO:

Every congregation has members who aren't able to attend regularly, usually for health reasons. Consider asking your pastor or a ministry leader if there's someone you can encourage.

If you aren't comfortable visiting in person, drop them a short note from time to time, or maybe send them a modest bouquet of flowers on special occasions.

REFLECTIONS

DAY 5 | JOURNAL:

Record prayers, thoughts, or insights from your time with God.

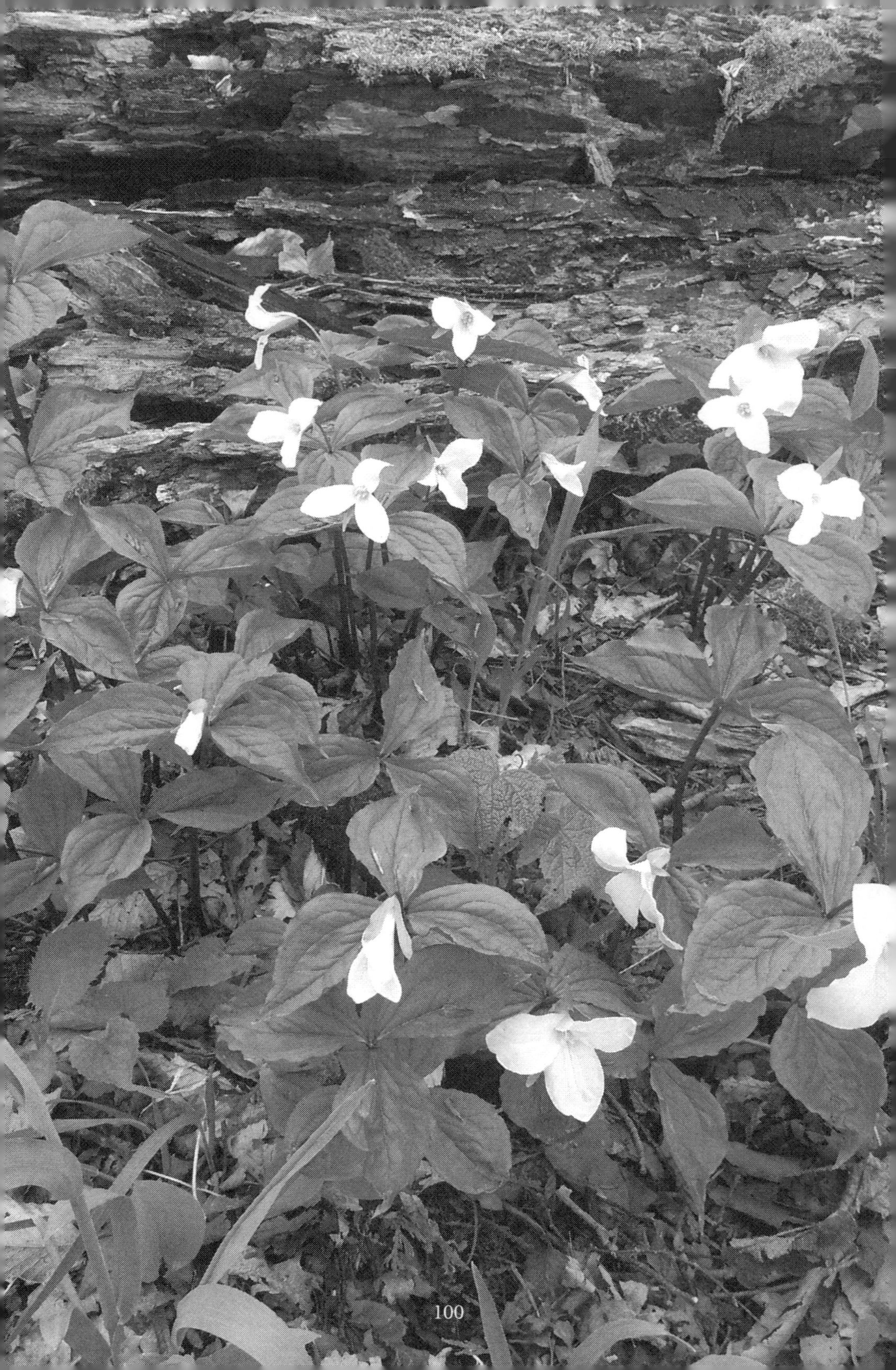

WEEK 25: FROM MANY TO ONE

CONSIDER:

Every spring, trilliums bloom under hardwood forest canopies across the nation. They pop up in small clusters and large colonies, dotting the woodlands with showy white blooms, nodding yellow blossoms, or deep red petals — depending on the variety. Each plant produces only one flower, but together, trilliums can create a sea of color.

What looks like many different plants on the surface is really one big, interconnected root below the soil. Trilliums spread most efficiently by sending out rhizomes — horizontal roots with little nodes that can send up new shoots for new plants, which is why you find them growing so close together.

Although each flower does produce a single seed, the odds of it germinating are slim. A seed only gets planted in the wild if a hungry ant steals it, eats the tasty (well, to an ant) coating, and discards it. Trilliums take almost as long as humans to reach adulthood. It takes about 10 years to produce a flower. In the meantime, it grows and matures in the company of its fellow trilliums.

The family of God is made up of many people rooted in the one true God. If you peek through the window of any given congregation on a Sunday morning, you won't see a uniform sea of people who all look, act, and think the same way. But you will see a spiritual family that has sprung up from "the root of Jesse" (Isaiah 11) — Jesus.

> *"Yet for us there is one God, the Father, of whom are all things, and we for Him; and one Lord Jesus Christ, through whom are all things, and through whom we live."*
> (1 Corinthians 8:6)

We are many fearfully and wonderfully made individuals who bring our varied personalities, experiences, gifts, and passions with us when we join God's family. Unlike trilliums, we shouldn't all look essentially the same. Our goal, as the body, should not be uniformity — trying to make everyone fit into our mold of what a good Christian should look like.

God created each one-of-a-kind individual to best serve His kingdom's purposes. We are one, finding unity in our common root: Christ. When we grow in close proximity to one another, we offer protection for those who are still maturing, companionship to those near us, and an opportunity to display all the beauty of our Lord for the world to see.

WEEK 25

DAY 1 | PRAY:

Help me live in harmony with others. Keep me from being haughty. Don't let me be wise in my own eyes. Rather than repaying evil for evil, help me do what is honorable in the sight of all. If possible, so far as it depends on me, I want to live peaceably with everyone. (Romans 12)

DAY 2 | MEMORIZE:

Galatians 3:26-27

For you are all sons of God through faith in Christ Jesus. For as many of you as were baptized into Christ have put on Christ.

DAY 3 | READ AND RESPOND:

Colossians 2:1-10

What is Paul's wish (and probably his prayer) for the Colossian church in verses 1-3?

_____
_____
_____

What warnings does Paul have for the church in this passage?

_____
_____
_____

According to these verses, how can we protect ourselves and others from spiritual pitfalls?

_____
_____
_____

What does the phrase *"complete in Him"* (verse 10) mean?

_____
_____
_____

DAY 4 | DO:

The next time you're at church or a church function, take a moment to look at the people you know and consider what they bring to the church. Would your church body function as well without them? What holes would they leave in your church's ministry?

REFLECTIONS

DAY 5 | JOURNAL:

Record prayers, thoughts, or insights from your time with God.

(Photo credit: © Ira Mark Rappaport / Adobe Stock)

WEEK 26: FROM PRETENDING TO AUTHENTICITY

CONSIDER:

When chickens are distressed, they raise a ruckus. One afternoon, I went to check on the flock's excessive squawking. Two beady, black eyes set close to a long, pink snout with wiggling whiskers stared out at me from under the coop. Last time I checked, possums were nocturnal. A midday egg raid meant he was hungry.

The possum and I had a brief stare-down before I grabbed a stick and made a mad dash in his direction. Bad decision! The poor thing collapsed when I charged it. He couldn't do any harm in his comatose condition, so I put down my stick and went back to my household chores.

I don't know about you, but I play possum at times. Rather than pretending I'm dead, however, I pretend all is well even though I'm spiritually comatose. Oh, Christ is still alive in me. But my spiritual senses are dull, I can't hear the voice of God, and I don't see the path my Shepherd is leading me along.

Others won't know we're dying inside if we pretend all is well. For our own sake and the sake of Christ's body, God wants us to put away our foolery and live honestly before one another. He wants us to quit pretending so we can journey forward together knowing *"no temptation has overtaken you except such as is common to man."* (1 Corinthians 10:13)

We all sin. We all struggle against our flesh to obey God. Telling our brothers and sisters in Christ that all is well, when in fact it's not, is a lie. Living as though we have it all together when we don't is a deception. Not only is it sinful, it leaves us all feeling as though we walk alone. We are all encouraged when we know we're in this together.

> *Therefore, putting away lying, "Let each one of you speak truth with his neighbor," for we are members of one another.* (Ephesians 4:25)

I'm not suggesting we unburden our souls to everyone. That would be unwise. There are appropriate times and people with whom to have honest conversations about our inner struggles — usually to encourage or comfort someone walking a similar path or seek godly advice. However, it blesses everyone when we admit we battle sin. It blesses the pray-er and the pray-ee when we ask others to intercede for us. That's why James exhorts us to *"confess your trespasses to one another, and pray for one another, that you may be healed."* (James 5:16)

DAY 1 | PRAY:

Lord, who may abide in your tabernacle? Who may dwell in your holy hill? You have promised eternity to those who walk upright, work righteously, and speak the truth in their hearts. Teach me to fear you and know your honor. (Psalm 15)

DAY 2 | MEMORIZE:

Luke 12:2

For there is nothing covered that will not be revealed, nor hidden that will not be known.

DAY 3 | READ AND RESPOND:

1 John 1:1-8

Is the eternal life that was manifested to us a something or a someone? What or who is it?

_____
_____
_____

In verses 3-4, why is John declaring what he has seen, heard, and touched?

_____
_____
_____

Why is walking in the light evidence that we have fellowship with God? Who else do we have fellowship with when we walk in the light?

_____
_____
_____

Who, besides us, is made a liar when we claim or pretend we don't sin?

_____
_____
_____

DAY 4 | DO:

Look at yourself in the mirror.

What do you see? Does the image of yourself change when you look more deeply at your inner self? If so, in what ways? Ask God for strength to win those inner battles. Ask someone you trust to pray for you, as well.

REFLECTIONS

DAY 5 | JOURNAL:

Record prayers, thoughts, or insights from your time with God.

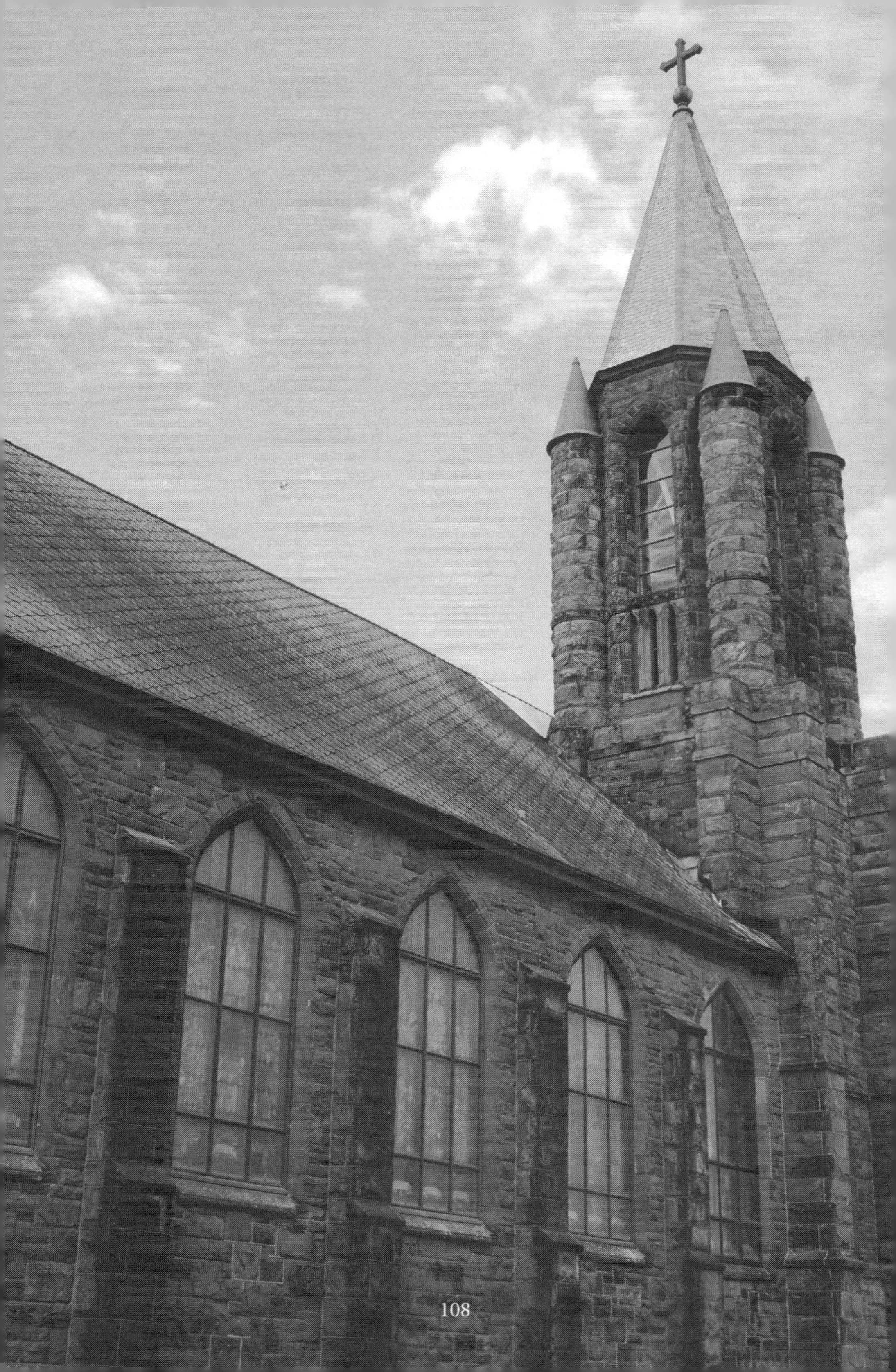

WEEK 27: FROM JUDGMENT TO GRACE

CONSIDER:

I was raised in a legalistic church. I'm thankful for the sound Bible teaching I received and for the people who shaped my childhood. But I grew up thinking Christianity was more about dos and don'ts than pursuing God. I was prideful about my Bible knowledge and good behavior. I was ungracious toward those who didn't measure up to my standards.

Then I grew, physically *and* spiritually. God peeled back the layers of my good behavior and showed me the rot in my heart. He reminded me that, were it not for His grace, I would suffer the penalty of His judgment, too — eternal death. If the holy God could show me grace, should I not, as a weak and sinful person, show grace to others?

At some point in my journey, I became a student of God's heart and He began cleaning up my sinful soul. Obeying the dos and don'ts wasn't a bad thing, but my motives were wrong. I wanted to make an impression on others rather than honor my Savior. Did He criticize and condemn me? No. He gently disciplined me, waited for me to leave my old ways behind, and led me to a better place.

Ephesians 5:1 instructs us to be imitators of God. Just as God shows us grace, the love of Christ compels us to show others grace. At my worst moments, I am most thankful for those who imitate God. They graciously and gently challenge me to live a holy life. Those who judge me only heap on more shame.

The key to being gracious rather than judgmental is being a student of God's Word *and* God's heart. If we get too wrapped up in the letter of the law, we miss the reason God gave us the law — to show us our need for a Savior. Though God will judge the unrepentant, His heart is full of grace toward all who call on His name.

A friend once said, "The church tends to shoot its wounded." It's sad but true. God is the Great Physician. When we move from judgment to grace in our earthly relationships, we bind up wounds rather than multiplying them. We put God's heart on display and bring Him glory.

The Lord is not slack concerning His promise, as some count slackness, but is longsuffering toward us, not willing that any should perish but that all should come to repentance. (2 Peter 3:9)

DAY 1 | PRAY:

Who am I to judge your servants, Lord? To you alone they stand or fall. Indeed, you are able to make them stand. Change my heart so I won't judge others anymore, but rather resolve this; not to put a stumbling block in my brother's way. (Romans 14)

DAY 2 | MEMORIZE:

Romans 14:4

Who are you to judge another's servant? To his own master he stands or falls. Indeed, he will be made to stand, for God is able to make him stand.

DAY 3 | READ AND RESPOND:

John 8:1-11

Why were the Pharisees judgmental toward the adulterous woman?

_____
_____
_____

How did Jesus help them replace their judgment with grace?

_____
_____
_____

Why do you think the oldest men were the first to leave?

_____
_____
_____

How did Jesus respond to the woman after everyone had left?

_____
_____
_____

DAY 4 | DO:

Do you know someone who needs a little extra measure of grace right now?

Paint a rock with an encouraging word on it and leave it, anonymously if you'd like, on their doorstep. My piano students did this for me once, and it made my day.

REFLECTIONS

DAY 5 | JOURNAL:

Record prayers, thoughts, or insights from your time with God.

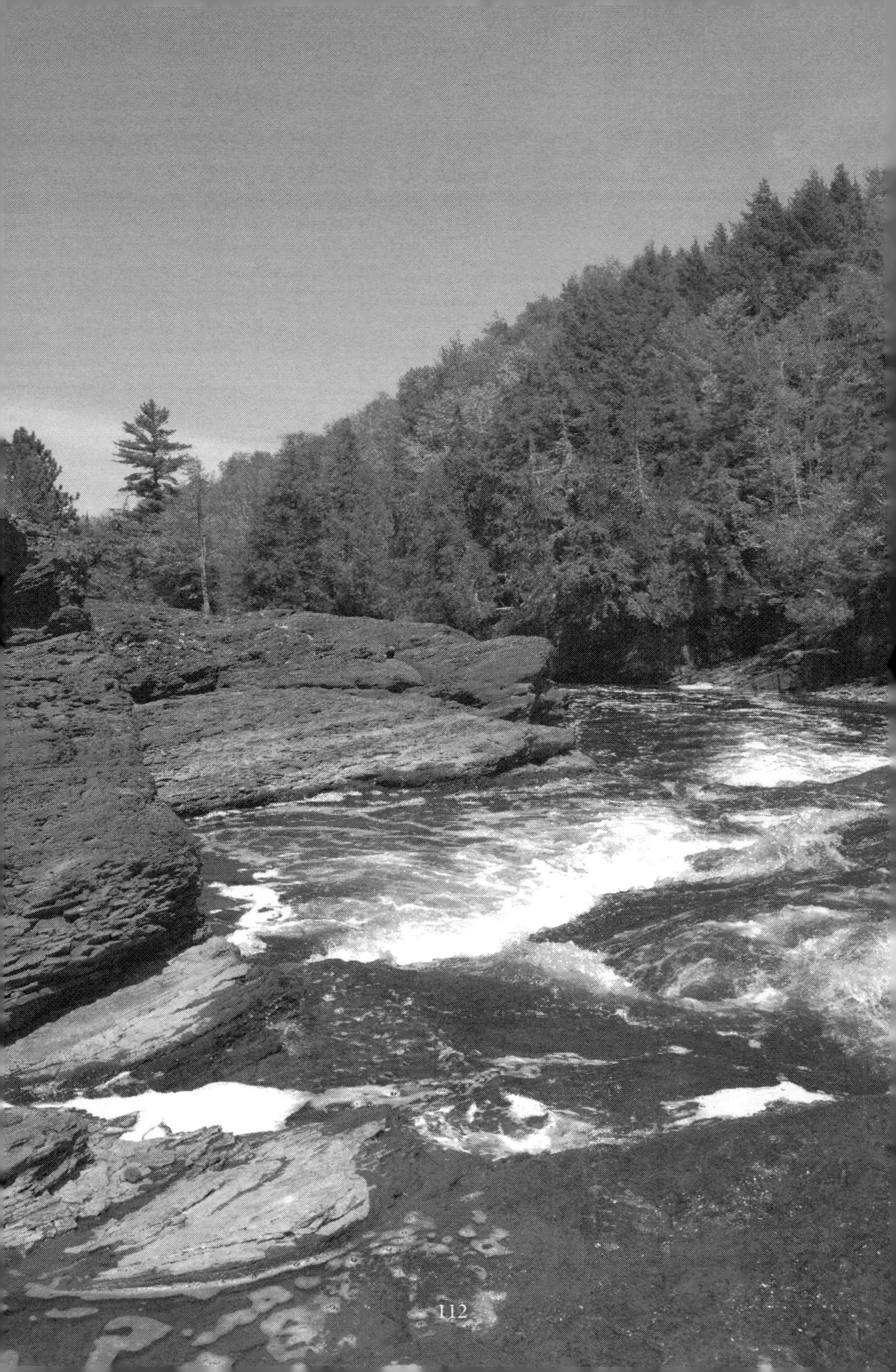

WEEK 28: FROM VENGEFUL TO MERCIFUL

CONSIDER:

There's a gorgeous little river in Wisconsin that runs north into Lake Superior. Its wild shores are dotted with old log estates and matching boathouses with canoes and kayaks, the only boats suited to this shallow and narrow river.

The Bois Brule has an unpredictable personality. One moment it's peaceful, the next it's rushing over swift rapids — trying to throw you into its icy waters. If you didn't know better, you'd think the river was trying to get even with you for disturbing it.

Getting even. Is there really such a thing? We've all been hurt by someone and wanted to inflict pain on them in return. We think it will make us feel better if they suffer like we did.

It doesn't work. Why? Because human vengeance contradicts God's laws. This is made clear in 1 Thessalonians 5:15: *"See that no one renders evil for evil to anyone."* There's no wiggle room in that command. We are not to seek vengeance when someone harms us. In fact, that verse goes on to say, *"But always pursue what is good both for yourselves and for all."*

How can we do good to those who have done evil to us? God gave us a way. By the power of the Holy Spirit, we can let Him handle it.

Vengeance is Mine, and recompense;
Their foot shall slip in due time;
For the day of their calamity is at hand,
And the things to come hasten upon them. (Deuteronomy 32:35)

God sees the injustices we suffer. Whether it seems like it or not, those who hurt us aren't getting away with *anything*. Oh, we may not see God's vengeance in the here and now, but He is our defender. He will avenge the wrongs committed against us.

Unless those who've wronged us seek God's mercy. Mercy is not getting what we deserve. We all deserve God's wrath and eternal banishment because we all fall short of God's glory. By the Spirit's power, we can pray for others to repent, to find God's mercy (as we have) rather than hoping for God's vengeance against them. While we wait, our assignment is to be a living testament to God's goodness.

You have heard that it was said, "You shall love your neighbor and hate your enemy." But I say to you, love your enemies, bless those who curse you, do good to those who hate you, and pray for those who spitefully use you and persecute you. (Matthew 5:43-44)

DAY 1 | PRAY:

You have shown me, O Lord, what is good. And what you require of me is to do justly, to love mercy, and to walk humbly with you. I want to invite your blessing by showing mercy to others. (Micah 6)

DAY 2 | MEMORIZE:

Matthew 5:7

Blessed are the merciful, for they shall obtain mercy.

DAY 3 | READ AND RESPOND:

Romans 12:9-21

Verse 9 says, *"Let love be without hypocrisy."*
How/why is seeking revenge hypocritical?

_____
_____
_____

There are many commands in these verses. Summarize how we should interact with one another in one sentence.

_____
_____
_____

How are we instructed to treat our enemies?

_____
_____
_____

Can you think of an example of good overcoming evil?

_____
_____
_____

DAY 4 | DO:

Make a list of all the instructions Paul gives us in Romans 12:9-21. Consider the areas where you are strong and the areas where you have room for growth. Look for opportunities to practice these things.

REFLECTIONS

DAY 5 | JOURNAL:

Record prayers, thoughts, or insights from your time with God.

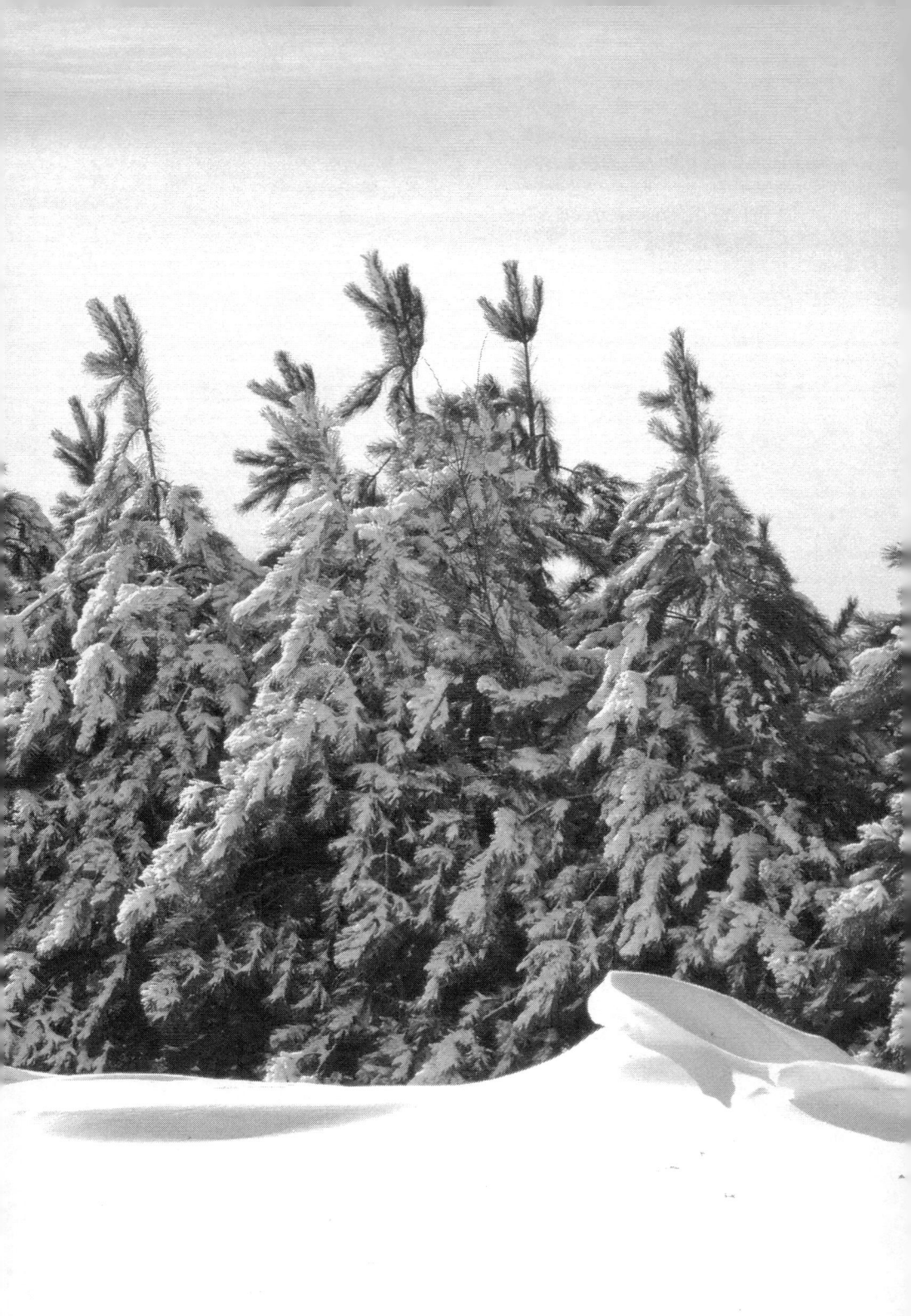

WEEK 29: FROM UNFORGIVING TO FORGIVING

CONSIDER:

A steady snow can gradually transform darkness to light. A layer of white builds up on the dark tree bark, the defunct corn stalks, and the exposed black earth. Everything outdoors looks fresh and clean. The snow hides the ugly imperfections of the season. God's visual aid shows the transformation of a dark heart taken to Christ's cross for cleansing.

Purify me with hyssop and I shall be clean; wash me and I shall be whiter than snow. (Psalm 51:7, NASB1995)

Whiter than snow... I wonder how *anything* could be whiter than snow. I wonder at how my wicked heart could be made so clean, not just once but over and over again — like each fresh snowfall — no matter how great the sin. I'm so thankful God's mercies are new *every morning*.

But it doesn't stop there. Just as we enjoy God's endless forgiveness toward us, His imperfect children, He assigns us the task of endlessly forgiving others. That gets tricky sometimes, doesn't it? People we trust disappoint and wound us. How can we forgive such betrayals?

I think it's helpful to look at things from a different vantage point. When we're sinned against, we tend to see the situation through our pain, through our indignation, through our sense of injustice. Do we consider the other person's perspective? God's perspective?

A good friend of mine says, "To know all is to forgive all." It has changed my perspective on conflicts, forgiveness, and reconciliation dramatically! To know all *is* to forgive all.

To know the freedom from guilt and shame found in God's forgiveness compels us to offer freedom to others. To know the joy of restored fellowship with God compels us to restore fellowship with one another after a conflict. To know a person's story, to understand why they are who they are, allows us to show them the same compassion God shows us. If a perfect, sinless God can forgive a bunch of hooligans like us, what's stopping us from forgiving the hooligans God has put in our lives?

God's commitment and call to reconciliation are clear. He made the way to restore our relationship with Him. He made forgiveness possible. In the Old Testament, this was done through the sacrificial system. In the New Testament, this was done through Christ's sacrifice on the cross. It is only through the power of the Holy Spirit that we can live as forgiven and forgiving people.

DAY 1 | PRAY:

Lord, let all bitterness, wrath, anger, clamor, and evil speaking be put away from me, along with all malice. Help me be kind to others, tenderhearted, forgiving others, even as God in Christ forgave me. (Ephesians 4)

DAY 2 | MEMORIZE:

Colossians 3:12-13

Therefore, as the elect of God, holy and beloved, put on tender mercies, kindness, humility, meekness, longsuffering; bearing with one another, and forgiving one another, if anyone has a complaint against another; even as Christ forgave you, so you also must do.

DAY 3 | READ AND RESPOND:

Leviticus 16:3-11

Why did Aaron (the priest) need a bull and two goats for the sin offering? What role did each play?

_____
_____
_____

The scapegoat was a picture of the coming Messiah. What similarities are there between the scapegoat and Jesus, as sin sacrifices?

_____
_____
_____

Why do we need God's forgiveness? Find a verse to support your answer.

_____
_____
_____

Is it sinful for us not to forgive others? Why or why not?

_____
_____

DAY 4 | DO:

Are you on bad terms with anyone? Begin praying God will give you the desire and the opportunity to forgive that person and restore your relationship. Then follow through by asking God for the strength to do it.

REFLECTIONS

DAY 5 | JOURNAL:

Record prayers, thoughts, or insights from your time with God.

(Photo credit: ©[Chris Hill] / Adobe Stock)

WEEK 30: FROM CRUEL TO KIND

CONSIDER:

Every spring, the healthy population of garter snakes at our local nature preserve comes out of hibernation. They form mating balls and slither down the hill. Each male is hoping to mate with the female in its ball. For garter snake males, the only risk is being rejected.

Green anacondas also form mating balls that can cling together for up to four weeks. The females give off alluring pheromones — at least male anacondas find them alluring. Up to a dozen males wrap themselves around a female, vying for her attention. She mates with several. Then she eats a couple. Nice, huh? She lures them in, lulls them into a false sense of security, then has them for lunch.

While we don't need to worry about cannibalism, we do risk exposing ourselves to cruelty when we engage with others. A quick look at history reminds us how unkind people can be. Consider medieval torture methods, the nine-plus million people Stalin starved out, or the evils inflicted in concentration camps. For that matter, five minutes in the average junior high classroom can reveal the unkindness in our human hearts.

But the heart transformed by God's love sees people through God's eyes. We find the desire to extend kindness to others. What makes one part of the body healthier makes the whole body healthier.

You know the old adage "Treat others the way you want to be treated"? Well, that's more than a quaint saying. It's a directive Jesus gave during the Sermon on the Mount:

Therefore, whatever you want men to do to you, do also to them, for this is the Law and the Prophets. (Matthew 7:12)

Kindness requires forethought, at times. It helps to step back and consider how we would like to be treated, then show the same consideration. A moment of reflection can spare us, and others, the damage of hasty, thoughtless words and hurtful actions.

Kindness is a thoughtful word, an encouraging smile, a hospitable home, or a helping hand. We can each find ways to pass God's kindness on to others, ways that tap into our natural talents and spiritual gifts. Why is showing kindness important? Because, according to Jesus, kindness is consistent with the Old Testament laws, the words of the prophets, and God's character.

He has told you, O man, what is good; and what does the Lord require of you but to do justice, and to love kindness, and to walk humbly with your God?
(Micah 6:8, ESV)

DAY 1 | PRAY:

A soft answer turns away wrath, but a harsh word stirs up anger, and the tongue of the wise uses knowledge rightly. Let the words of my mouth and the meditation of my heart be pleasing to you, O Lord, my strength and my Redeemer. (Proverbs 15, Psalm 19)

DAY 2 | MEMORIZE:

Proverbs 21:21 (ESV)

Whoever pursues righteousness and kindness will find life, righteousness, and honor.

DAY 3 | READ AND RESPOND:

Luke 10:30-37

What happened to the man traveling to Jericho in this parable?
_____
_____

How did the priest and Levite respond when they saw him? What reasons might they give for responding this way?
_____
_____
_____

What kindnesses did the Samaritan show this man?
_____
_____

Based on Jesus' words in verses 36-37, how would He want us to respond in this situation?
_____
_____
_____
_____

DAY 4 | DO:

Watch for opportunities to do random acts of kindness for strangers. It can be something as simple as holding the door for someone or letting them go ahead of you in the checkout line. What was the outcome of your kindness?

REFLECTIONS

DAY 5 | JOURNAL:

Record prayers, thoughts, or insights from your time with God.

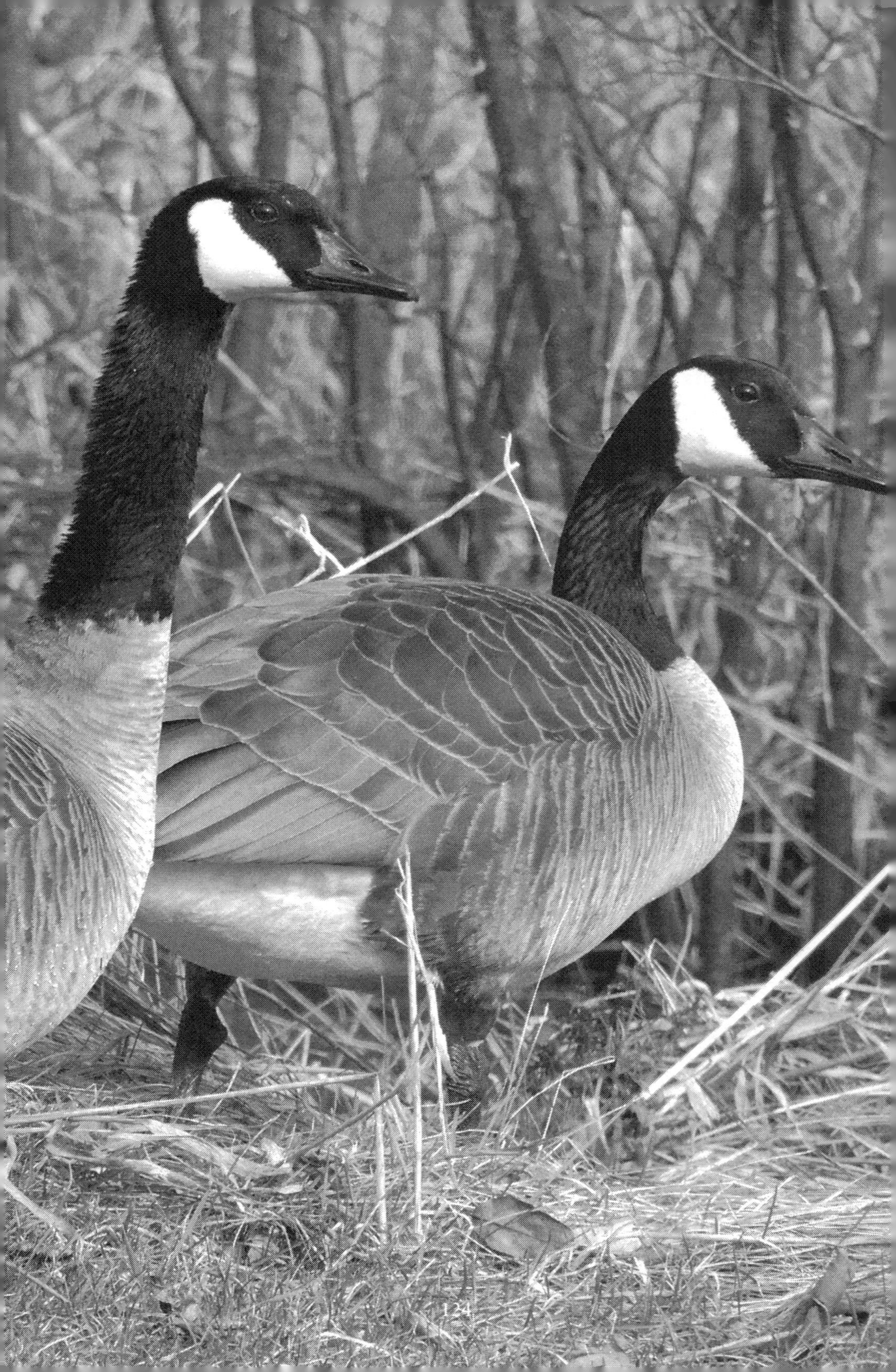

WEEK 31: FROM SELFISH TO SELFLESS

CONSIDER:

One fall night, an unfamiliar call drew my attention toward a pregnant moon. Six snow geese flew before the full moon, their graceful white flight illuminated by its soft light. I will not easily forget that sight or the soothing song they sang.

Snow geese don't often pass this way. Their Canadian cousins, however, come through in droves. On high-traffic days, their lopsided Vs dot the horizon as far as the eye can see. They call out instructions and greet each other in loud, nasal voices.

If you watch geese fly for any length of time, you'll see their formations morph. Certain geese move backward or forward in line. The strongest geese take turns leading. These fellows break the wind so the weaker geese can draft, like a Metro behind a semi, and make the arduous 2,000-mile journey. Tired geese move to the back for a little rest.

Geese are devoted to one another. The strong watch out for the weak. An injured or ill goose is never left alone. The flock might move on but its mate or a companion will stay behind until it is either able to fly or dies.

Our siblings in Christ can add joy to our arduous journey. As we gather and greet one another on Sunday mornings, for small groups or for social events, we encourage each other along the way.

At some points, we're strong. We're able to help the flock, making the way easier for the young, the struggling, or the infirmed. We lend our strength so their weakness doesn't prevent them from going on. We support those who are wounded or ill. We wait with them until they have the strength to go on or God takes them eternally home.

Now we exhort you, brethren, warn those who are unruly, comfort the fainthearted, uphold the weak, be patient with all. (1 Thessalonians 5:14)

At other points in our journey, we're weak. It's our turn to drop back and regain our strength. Our illness, wounds, or burdens may even ground us. This allows others to lend us their strength. As they wait with us, supporting us until we are strong again or God calls us home, we bless each other and glorify our Heavenly Father.

We who are strong ought to bear with the failings of the weak and not to please ourselves. Each of us should please our neighbors for their good, to build them up. (Romans 15:1-2, NIV)

WEEK 31

DAY 1 | PRAY:

Lord, change my heart so I do nothing out of selfish ambition or vain conceit. Rather, in humility let me value others above myself, not looking to my own interests but to the interests of the others. (Philippians 2)

DAY 2 | MEMORIZE:

Ezekial 34:15-16a

"I will feed My flock, and I will make them lie down," says the Lord God. "I will seek what was lost and bring back what was driven away, bind up the broken and strengthen what was sick."

DAY 3 | READ AND RESPOND:

1 Kings 17:8-24

What did the widowed woman do to help Elijah? Why was she hesitant to do it?

_____
_____
_____

What did Elijah do to help the woman?

_____
_____
_____

Who did Elijah lend his strength to?

_____
_____
_____

In what ways did God prove Himself mighty in this story? How was He glorified?

_____
_____
_____

DAY 4 | DO:

We're all selfish by nature. It takes divine strength and sincere desire to put others first. Look for opportunities in the coming days to prioritize the needs and wants of others over your own. How was God honored by your actions? Were you and the person/people you prioritized encouraged? In what ways?

REFLECTIONS

DAY 5 | JOURNAL:

Record prayers, thoughts, or insights from your time with God.

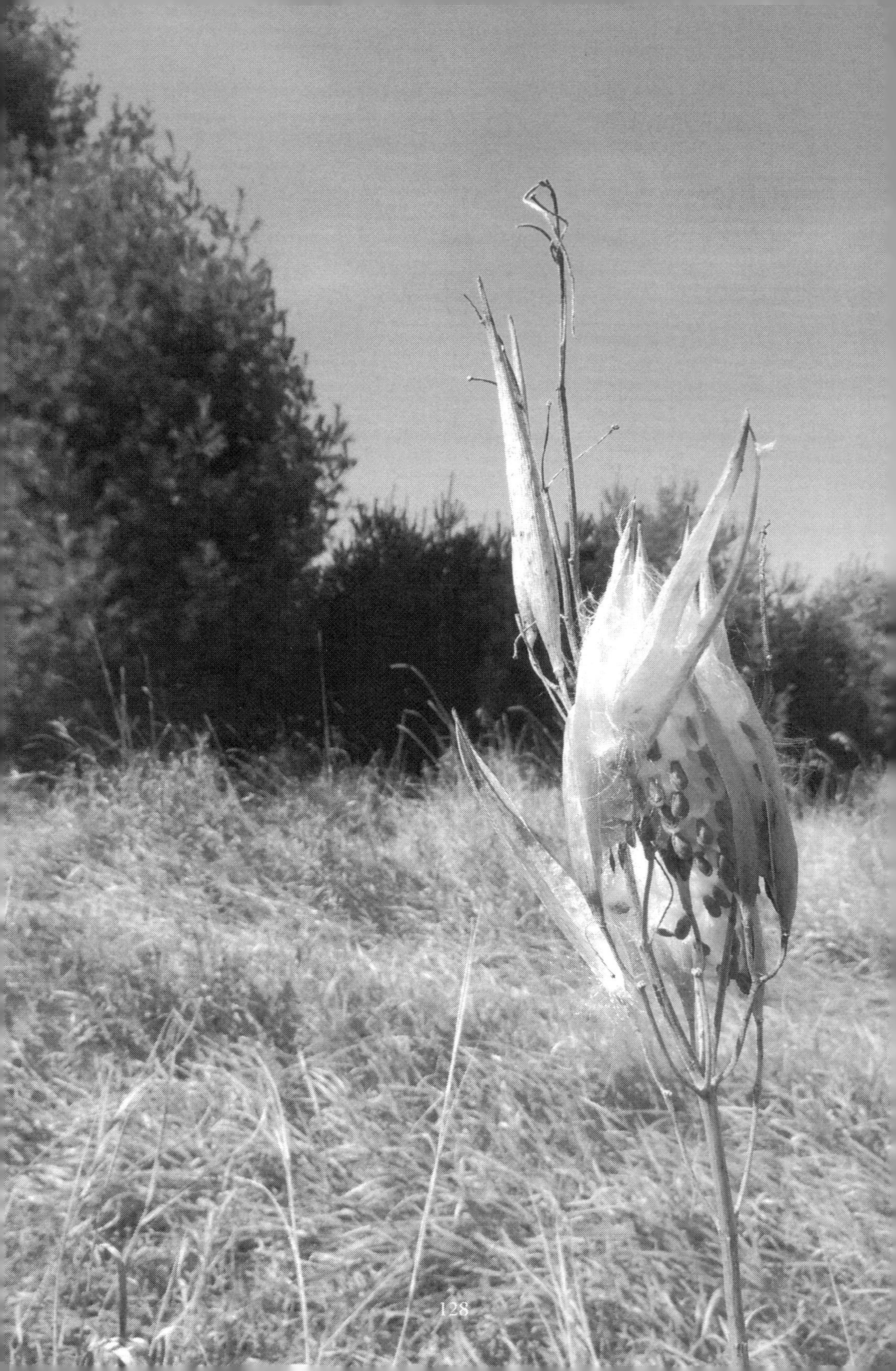

WEEK 32: FROM SOWING TO REAPING

CONSIDER:

After a long, warm autumn, the seed beans are dry. Some of the thin, brown pods crackle and pop open as I pick them, spilling their precious cargo on the cold, black earth. I hunt down the speckled ivory seeds as best I can.

Seeds are amazing. God made them in all shapes, sizes, and colors. Then He equipped them to spread in different ways. Spring-loaded seeds spray everywhere when the pod dries. Clinging seeds piggyback from place to place. Parachute seeds ride the wind to remote locations. Many seeds simply fall. Some germinate readily, while others are more reluctant. Jack pine cones, for instance, stay tightly closed until the heat from a forest fire forces them to drop their seeds on the scorched earth.

Believers, like seeds, come in all shapes, sizes, and colors. With their varying personalities come different approaches to spreading faith seeds. Some spring at every opportunity to proclaim the good news. Some build relationships with nonbelievers and demonstrate Christ's love. Others carry the gospel seeds as they fly to remote corners of the world. Many drop their seeds in their own neighborhoods and watch them grow. Then there are the jack pines (myself included) — reluctant souls who only sow God's Word when the heat is on.

There's one thing every seed has in common. It must die to live. When a seed germinates, a shoot breaks through the seed's outer coat. The plant lifts its leafy arms toward the sunlight. If properly nourished, it will grow, bloom, and set seeds of its own. And the original seed? It gives its life force to the new plant and the outer husk rots away. It dies to its old self and takes on a new living nature.

> *For whoever wishes to save his life will lose it, but whoever loses his life for my sake, he is the one who will save it.* (Luke 9:24)

Once we die to ourselves, God asks us to follow Him into the fields where *"the harvest is plentiful but the laborers are few."* (Matthew 9:37)

We aren't just seed sowers, we're also crop harvesters. Even though we live in an increasingly anti-Christian culture, souls are hungry for Christ. They may not know who they're looking for, but they feel the void inside. They pursue money, status, material goods, or fame. And if they attain their dream? The emptiness inside remains. Let's offer them the hope found through new life in Jesus.

DAY 1 | PRAY:

Lord, my desire is to sow righteousness and reap in mercy. Break up the fallow ground in my heart. It's time to seek you until you come and rain righteousness on me. (Hosea 10)

DAY 2 | MEMORIZE:

Galatians 6:8

For *he who sows to his flesh will of the flesh reap corruption, but he who sows to the Spirit will of the Spirit reap everlasting life.*

DAY 3 | READ AND RESPOND:

Luke 8:1-15

In this parable, what or whom do the seeds represent?

_____
_____
_____

Does every seed that's sown germinate? Why or why not?

_____
_____
_____

What four reasons does Jesus give for gospel seeds not germinating or growing?

_____
_____
_____

What sort of seed and seed sower are you?

_____
_____
_____

DAY 4 | DO:

Grow something. Plant a seed and watch it grow. Nurture it properly. What happens when it is deprived of water and light? What happens when people are deprived of the Living Water and the Light of the World?

REFLECTIONS

DAY 5 | JOURNAL:

Record prayers, thoughts, or insights from your time with God.

(Photo credit: © litsmejust / Adobe Stock)

WEEK 33: FROM SERVING TO BEING SERVED

CONSIDER:

I'm in the late fall of my life, sliding rapidly down the frosty slope toward winter. As I age, my mind and body continue to decline. I'm more forgetful. Learning new tricks is harder. I'm less agile and more fragile than in my younger years.

These God-ordained changes aren't always easy to accept. I've always done for others, caring for my friends, my family, and my church as God prompted me through the gifts He gave me. I taught piano lessons, cooked in camp kitchens, changed diapers in the church nursery, and sang in the choir.

For you, brethren, have been called to liberty; only do not use liberty as an opportunity for the flesh, but through love serve one another. (Galatians 5:13)

I still serve others. But as I'm slowing down, I'm also learning to let others serve me. After all, the command is to serve one another. We will not always be on the giving end of service, nor on the receiving end of service. We bless others when we serve them. We also bless others when we, with a humble and grateful heart, allow them to obey God's promptings and serve us.

Serving others teaches us humility. It reminds us the Lord of All wrapped a towel around His waist, filled a basin with water, and washed His disciples' feet just hours before He walked the lonely road to the cross — and finished His greatest act of service to all mankind. If we are leaders in our churches, ministries, jobs, or homes, we are not called to lord it over others. We are called to serve them.

But he who is greatest among you shall be your servant. (Matthew 23:11)

Being served by other people also teaches us humility. Sometimes God sends someone to fill a basin with water and wash our feet in His place. When we are weak, vulnerable, or can't do for ourselves, we're not called to fiercely defend our self-sufficiency. We are called to allow others to serve us. When we serve, we will be served in return. It's all part of God's grand design for His body.

The generous soul will be made rich, and he who waters will also be watered himself. (Proverbs 11:25)

Humbly serving and being served deals pride an oft-needed blow. Furthermore, the church is blessed, Christ's heart is expressed, and God is glorified.

DAY 1 | PRAY:

Lord, I have received a spiritual gift from you. Give me opportunities to minister to others with it, as a good steward of your grace, which comes to me in various ways. For even your Son did not come to be served, but to serve, and to give His life as a ransom for many. (1 Peter 4, Mark 10)

DAY 2 | MEMORIZE:

Hebrews 6:10

For God is not unjust to forget your work and labor of love which you have shown toward His name, in that you have ministered to the saints, and do minister.

DAY 3 | READ AND RESPOND:

1 Peter 4:7-11

How does fervently loving one another cover a multitude of sins? (Consider 1 Corinthians 13:1-13)

_____
_____

Why is hospitality mentioned in a passage about loving and serving one another? Why do you think Peter mentioned *"without grumbling"* in this directive?

_____
_____

Based on this passage, do you think everyone's acts of service will look or be the same? Why or why not?

_____
_____

What gifts and opportunities has God given you to serve? What has He given to others to serve you?

_____
_____

DAY 4 | DO:

Look for two opportunities in the upcoming days: one to serve someone else and one to allow someone else to serve you. Consider how you feel in each of these situations. Consider how the other person feels in each of these situations. Does this change your outlook on either serving or being served?

REFLECTIONS

DAY 5 | JOURNAL:

Record prayers, thoughts, or insights from your time with God.

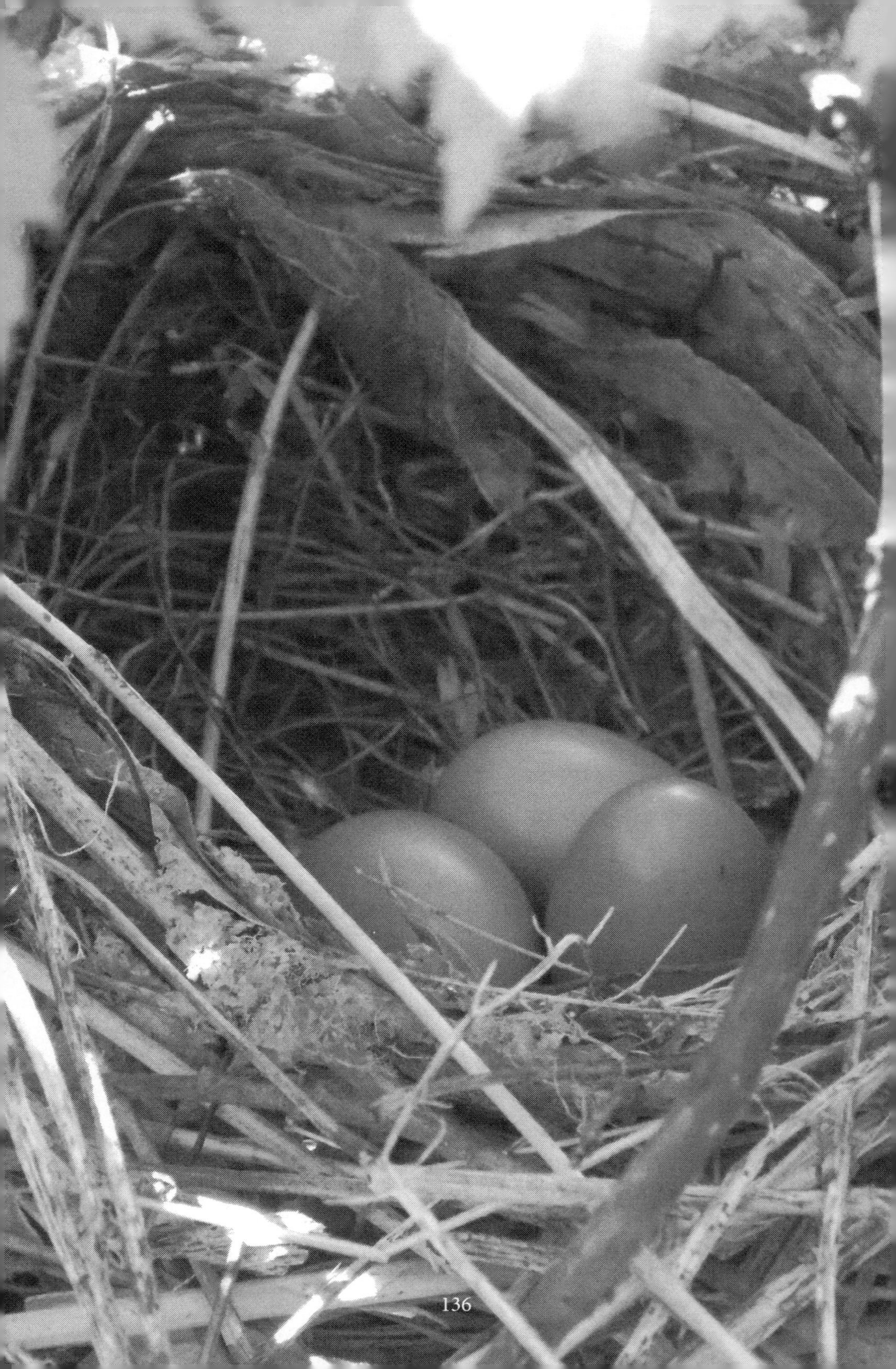

WEEK 34: FROM FULL QUIVER TO EMPTY NEST

CONSIDER:

Have you ever considered that God only loans us our children? They're really not ours to keep. He knew them before we took our first breath and will care for them after we have breathed our last. Having an empty nest drives this reality home.

My husband and I raised four children. It took 35 years to prepare them all for life and send them on their way. Furthermore, we homeschooled. There were always kids underfoot. There were field trips to organize, lessons to teach, meals to cook, household chores to complete, and church services to attend. Our house was busy, noisy, and chaotic.

We are enjoying a new household season. The calm and quiet came on gradually as, one by one, our children moved on to adulthood. As they matured, our relationships changed as well. We instructed and corrected them less. We had more discussions. Advice replaced directives as they gained confidence to make their own choices and accept the consequences — both good and bad.

Do not be deceived, God is not mocked; for whatever a man sows, that he will also reap. For he who sows to his flesh will of the flesh reap corruption, but he who sows to the Spirit will of the Spirit reap everlasting life. (Galatians 6:7-8)

Ideally, our children never depart from their godly training. Some do, some don't. Most go through rebellious seasons, exploring things that promise satisfaction and pleasure while questioning things they once accepted as truth.

Some find their way back to God rather quickly. Honestly, some never seem to find their way back, though only God knows the true condition of each soul. Still others are old before they figure out Jesus is *"the way, the truth, and the life."* (John 14:6) They exhaust all other options before finding completeness the only place it can be found — at the cross. They experience the pitfalls of alternate philosophies firsthand and suffer bitter disappointments before they *"taste and see that the Lord is good."* (Psalm 34:8) It's heartbreaking to watch, but we can have confidence in this: God is working out His sovereign will.

When our full quiver becomes an empty nest, we no longer have daily input in our kids' lives. But we have the power of prayer.

The Lord is far from the wicked,
But He hears the prayer of the righteous. (Proverbs 15:29)

We can pray with confidence in the One whose love for our children exceeds our own.

DAY 1 | PRAY:

Lord, if sinners entice my children, I pray they would not consent, that they would not walk in the way with them. Keep their feet from the path to evil. I pray they will listen to you, dwell safely, and will be secure, without fear of evil. (Proverbs 1)

DAY 2 | MEMORIZE:

Deuteronomy 6:6-7

And these words which I command you today shall be in your heart. You shall teach them diligently to your children, and shall talk of them when you sit in your house, when you walk by the way, when you lie down, and when you rise up.

DAY 3 | READ AND RESPOND:

Matthew 18:1-8

Why did Jesus say we must become like little children before we can enter His kingdom?

_____
_____
_____

How does Matthew 18:5 parallel Matthew 25:40?

_____
_____
_____

What warning does Jesus give to those who harm and mislead children?

_____
_____
_____

What do we learn about God's character in this passage?

_____
_____
_____

WEEK 34

DAY 4 | DO:

Find an age-appropriate way to encourage each of your children this week. If you have no children of your own, encourage a child who is special to you. Children, even adult children, need to know they are loved.

REFLECTIONS

DAY 5 | JOURNAL:

Record prayers, thoughts, or insights from your time with God.

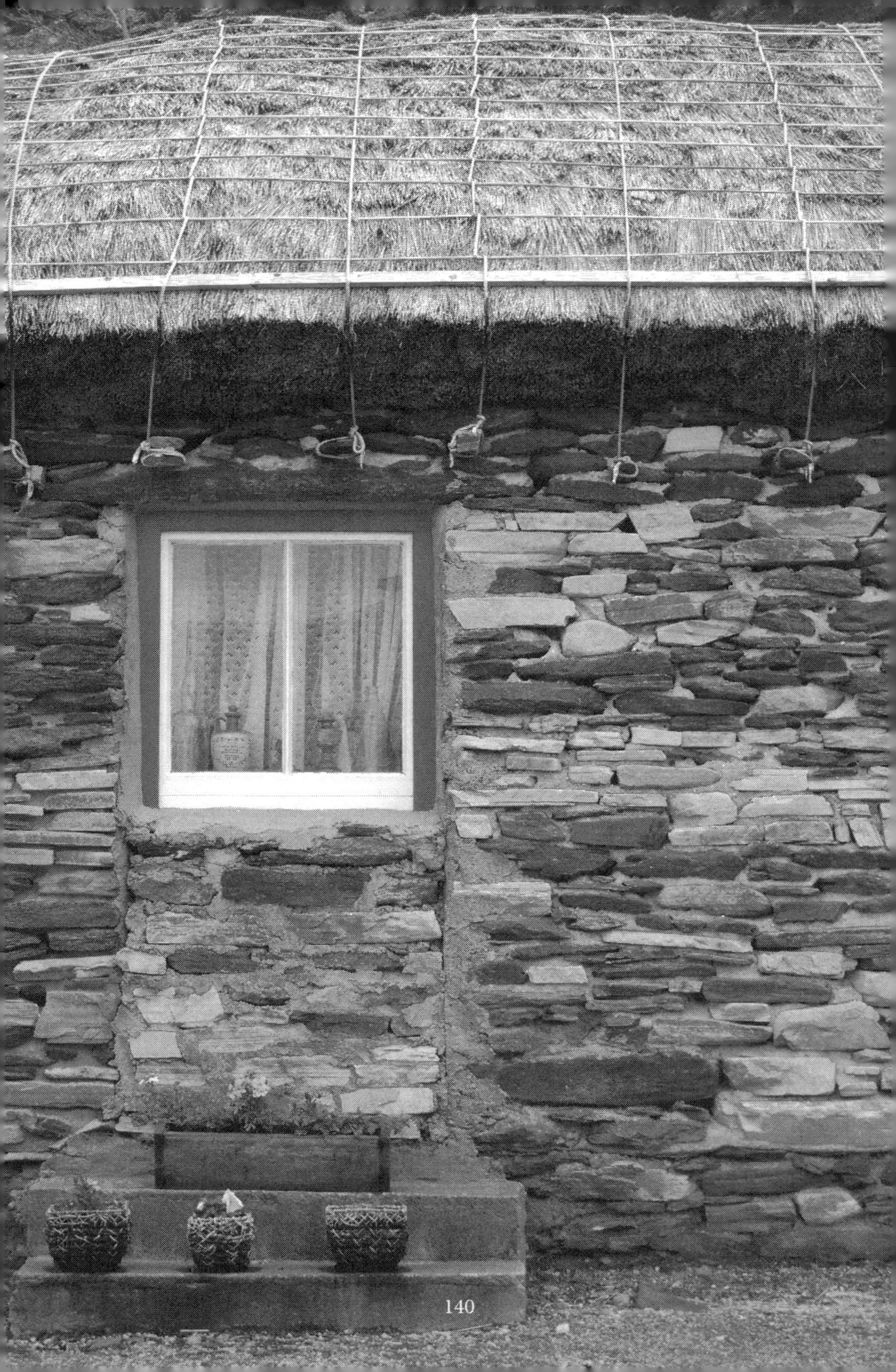

WEEK 35: FROM CURSED TO BLESSED

CONSIDER:

From time to time, I get the urge to work on my family tree. I can see how deep some of my roots go, but from my viewpoint, others look shallow. That may change as I continue to dig. While I research, I look for not only genetic links but spiritual links — evidence of God's hand at work through the generations.

My father's family is a bit of a mystery. It appears my paternal grandmother was a first-generation believer who gave her life to Christ as an adult. My grandpa became a Christian just three years before he passed away. My grandma faithfully followed Christ, raised godly children, and served her nonbelieving husband for years. God honored her faithfulness.

My mother's family is easier to trace. Both of my maternal grandparents were believers raised in Christian homes. At least two of my ancestors were Mennonites who moved to Pennsylvania to escape persecution and to worship freely.

People often quote Deuteronomy 5:9, where God says the sins of the fathers will keep cropping up for three to four generations. It's a sobering thought and a sound warning to live well. We all have personal sin-bents we don't want to pass on to our children, grandchildren, great-grandchildren, and great-great-grandchildren.

But Deuteronomy 5:10 seems to get overlooked. That's where God says He extends His compassion to a thousand generations of those who honor Him. As Deuteronomy 7:9 puts it:

Therefore know that the Lord your God, He is God, the faithful God who keeps covenant and mercy for a thousand generations with those who love Him and keep His commandments.

The unfathomable depths of God's love and mercy are truly awesome. His judgment against evil has a four-generation shelf life. That's a long time. But His blessings for righteousness won't expire for a thousand generations. He blesses obedience *250 times longer* than He curses rebellion.

I am eleven generations removed from my ancestors who left Europe in the face of persecution to freely pursue God. Who knows how many generations before them were sincere believers? I only know I reap the benefits of a godly heritage.

Whatever our individual stories, we can leave behind the fruit of lives devoted to prayer; lives of obedience inspired by God's unfailing love and incomprehensible holiness; lives filled with stories of God's faithfulness; and lives of worship and praise.

DAY 1 | PRAY:

Oh Lord, do not hold my former sins against me! Let your tender mercies come quickly to meet me, for I am in desperate need. Help me, O God of my salvation, for the glory of your name. Deliver me for your name's sake! (Psalm 78)

DAY 2 | MEMORIZE:

Psalm 71:18

Now also when I am old and gray-headed,
O God, do not forsake me,
Until I declare Your strength to this generation,
Your power to everyone who is to come.

DAY 3 | READ AND RESPOND:

Ephesians 1:15-23

What is Paul's prayer request for the Ephesian believers in verse 17?

_____
_____
_____

In verse 18, Paul explains why this is his prayer for the church. What is his reason?

_____
_____
_____

What is our inheritance as God's children?

_____
_____
_____

Would this be an effective and appropriate way to pray for our children? Why or why not?

_____
_____
_____

DAY 4 | DO:

Begin a journal for your children and future generations. Keep a record of answered prayers, unexpected blessings, and acts that demonstrate God's goodness toward you.

REFLECTIONS

DAY 5 | JOURNAL:

Record prayers, thoughts, or insights from your time with God.

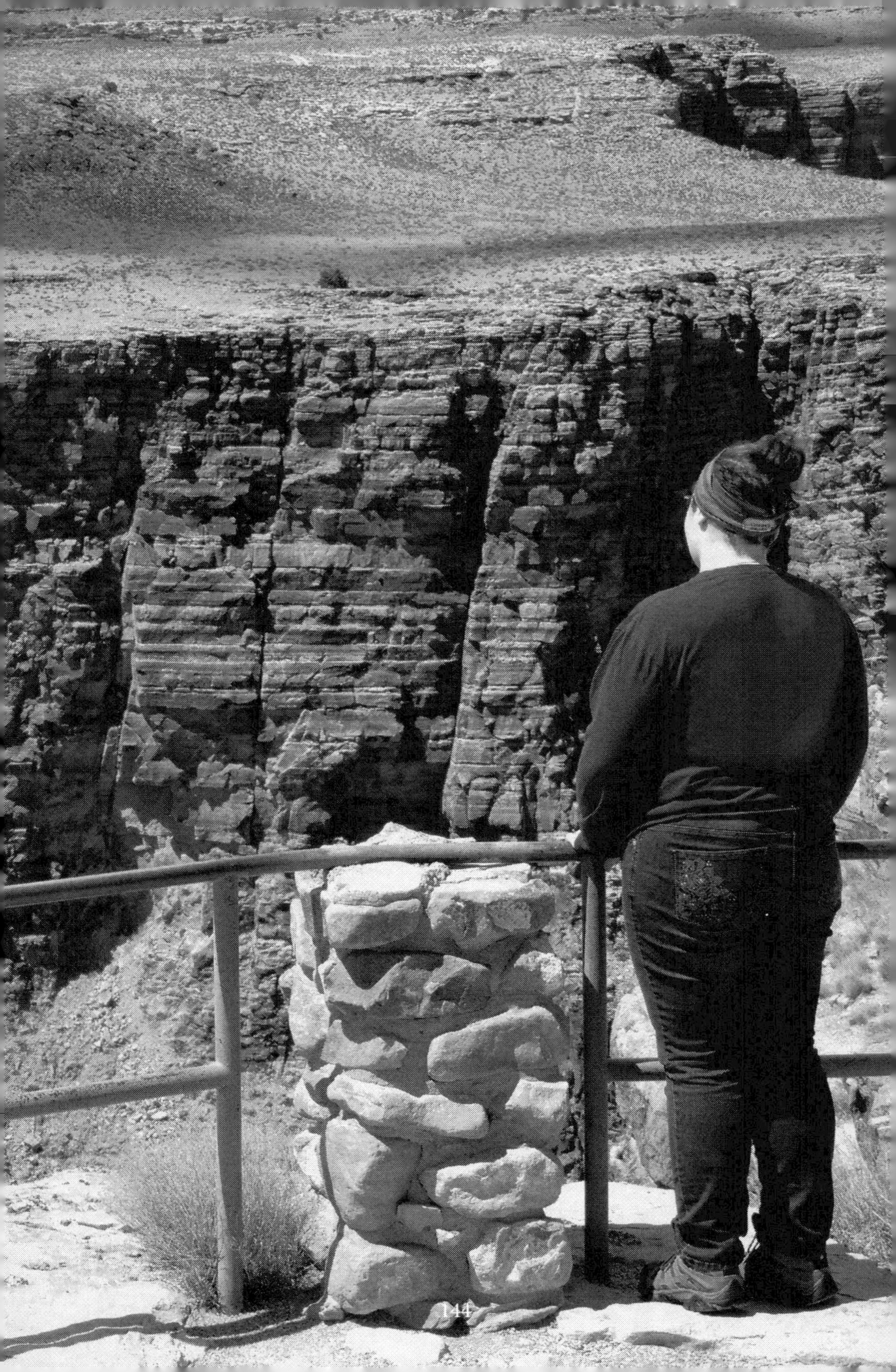

WEEK 36: FROM MISUNDERSTOOD TO FULLY KNOWN

CONSIDER:

I'm a bit of a misfit in my family, at least among the females. I see the world through a different lens. It's hard being misunderstood. They are professional career women, aware of the image they present to the outside world. They are always presentable, appropriate, and well-adapted to societal expectations.

I, on the other hand, got a healthy dose of my grandpa's hillbilly ways. He was seldom well-adapted to societal expectations, and I loved him for it. He was true to himself — a humble, barefooted farmer with day-old whiskers and onion breath, take it or leave it. I always admired him for his bold, honest way of life. I decided I also wanted to live true to myself, take it or leave it.

Following Grandpa's lead took me down a different path. Instead of pursuing a career, I homeschooled. Instead of dolling up to go out, I dressed down and gardened, barefooted. Makeup and jewelry became optional. I drew the line at peeling raw onions and eating them like apples, though.

The women in my family misjudge me. They question my motives and my actions. They read things into my words. Why? Because they cannot see my heart.

We all feel misunderstood at times. It's painful when others don't perceive us as we are. We're each a cocktail of experiences, perspectives, talents, and dreams. Each of our lives has a singular flavor no one else can replicate. We want someone to know and love the "real" us. But no one can see our true hearts.

Except the One who sees it all — all our thoughts, all our actions, and all our motives. Having taken a good, hard look at our unsavory ways, God still extends His love to us. We are fully known and fully accepted by our Creator. We can find comfort knowing He always understands us.

But then I will know fully just as I also have been fully known. (1 Corinthians 13:12b)

Life circumstances can leave us feeling alone, even in a crowd. We can find ourselves in a spiritual mire. When we cry out for help, our friends may fail us because they cannot see our dire situation. But God knows. What an amazing truth! The Lord of the universe understands our heart's cry even when we can't find words. Our Heavenly Father is always near, eager to lift us from our spiritual mire. He never fails us.

DAY 1 | PRAY:

Lord, you have tested my heart. You have visited me in the night. You have tried me and have found nothing. By the word of your lips, I have kept away from the paths of the destroyer. Uphold my steps in your paths, that my footsteps may not slip. (Psalm 17)

DAY 2 | MEMORIZE:

Psalm 139:1-3

O Lord, You have searched me and known me.
You know my sitting down and my rising up;
You understand my thought afar off.
You comprehend my path and my lying down,
And are acquainted with all my ways.

DAY 3 | READ AND RESPOND:

Psalm 139

Are you, like David, amazed by how completely God knows you (verse 6)? Why or why not?

_____
_____

Have you ever tried hiding from God, even though you knew it was impossible? What was the outcome?

_____
_____
_____

In verses 13-16, what truth comforts you the most?

_____
_____

Why does David ask God to search his heart and know his mind when he's already stated God knows everything?

_____
_____

DAY 4 | DO:

Get to know someone you care about a little better. Think of something new you'd like to know about the person. Think of something new you'd like to tell the person about yourself. Exchange your best memories, most embarrassing moments, or silliest mistakes — whatever you think will help you grow closer.

REFLECTIONS

DAY 5 | JOURNAL:

Record prayers, thoughts, or insights from your time with God.

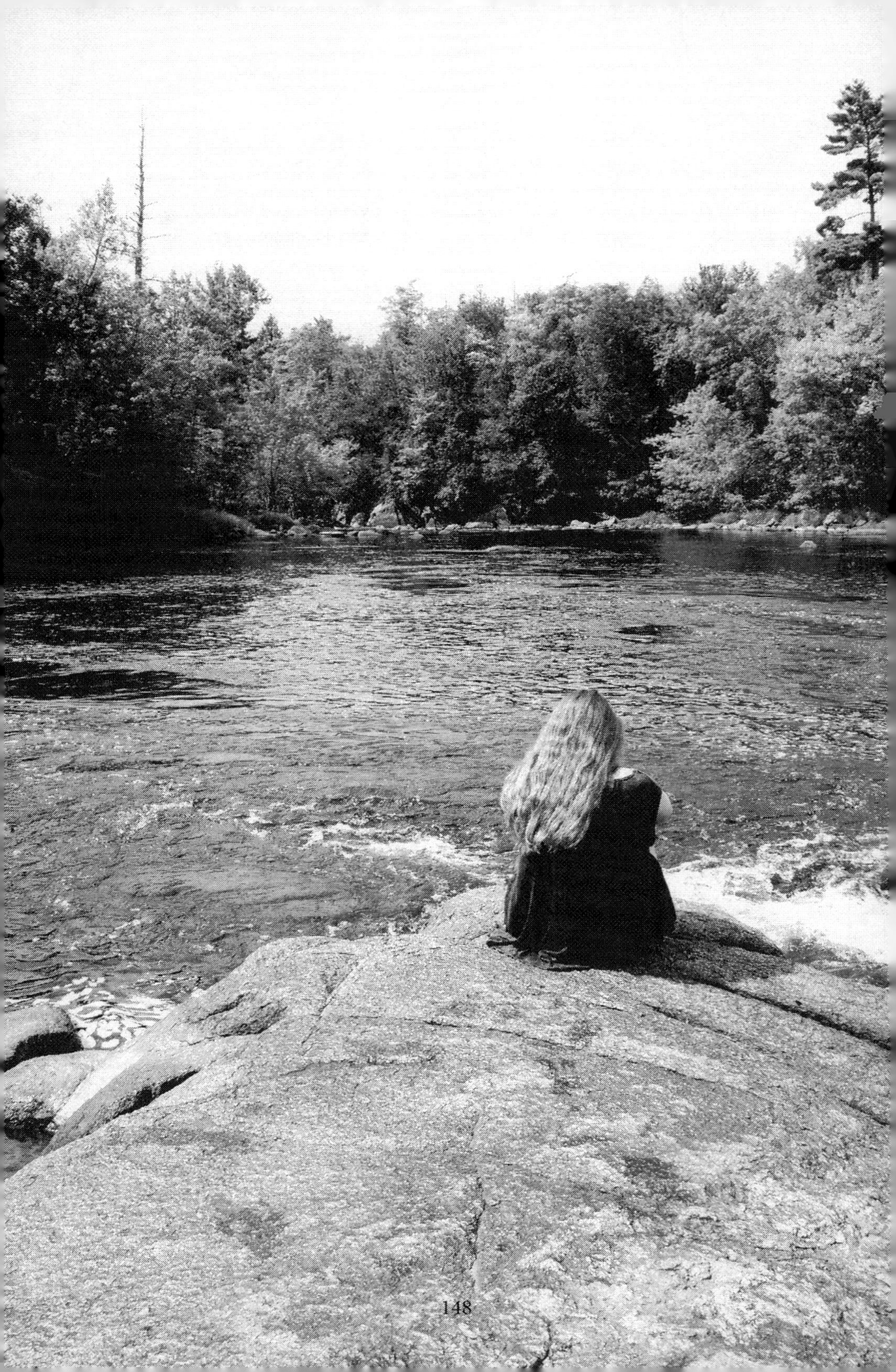

JOURNEYING WITH SELF (WEEKS 37-52)

As I live between the now and the not yet, I am often my own worst enemy. Even when my relationships with God and those around me are as serene as a summer lake at dawn, there are often gale-force winds making surfable waves inside me. The battle isn't just against the external forces of this world, the prince of this world (Satan), or his cohorts (demons). It's also an internal war against my flesh. It's against sin in me. It's against the recordings in my head, messages from past conversations and experiences. The Bible proclaims me a new creation in Christ, but I don't always believe it. If I did, I wouldn't talk, think, and act the way I sometimes do.

It takes a conscientious commitment to renew our minds daily, to replace those old lies with new truths. Sadly, we can't just hit the "delete" button and erase what's negatively shaped our thinking. But we can record over those messages. We can replace Satan's lies with God's living words — words with the power to help us see ourselves as God sees us: imperfect but precious, broken but restored, weak but invaluable.

Memorizing Bible verses is a crucial part of mind renewal. I can't tell you how many times I've quoted *"I discipline my body and bring it into subjection, lest, when I have preached to others, I myself should become disqualified"* (1 Corinthians 9:27) as I've walked through the grocery store bakery with an almond bear claw calling my name. I've reminded myself, when Satan dredges up sins God has long forgotten, the devil is *"the accuser of our brethren, who accuses them before our God day and night."* (Revelation 12:10) God's Word is our sword. With it, we can strike down the enemy.

On our way to what will be, our Father longs for us to joyfully sojourn with Him. Until then, the path will be riddled with rocks and roots that trip us up. We will fall flat on our faces from time to time. Still, God promises, *"Peace I leave with you, My peace I give to you; not as the world gives do I give to you. Let not your heart be troubled, neither let it be afraid."* (John 14:27)

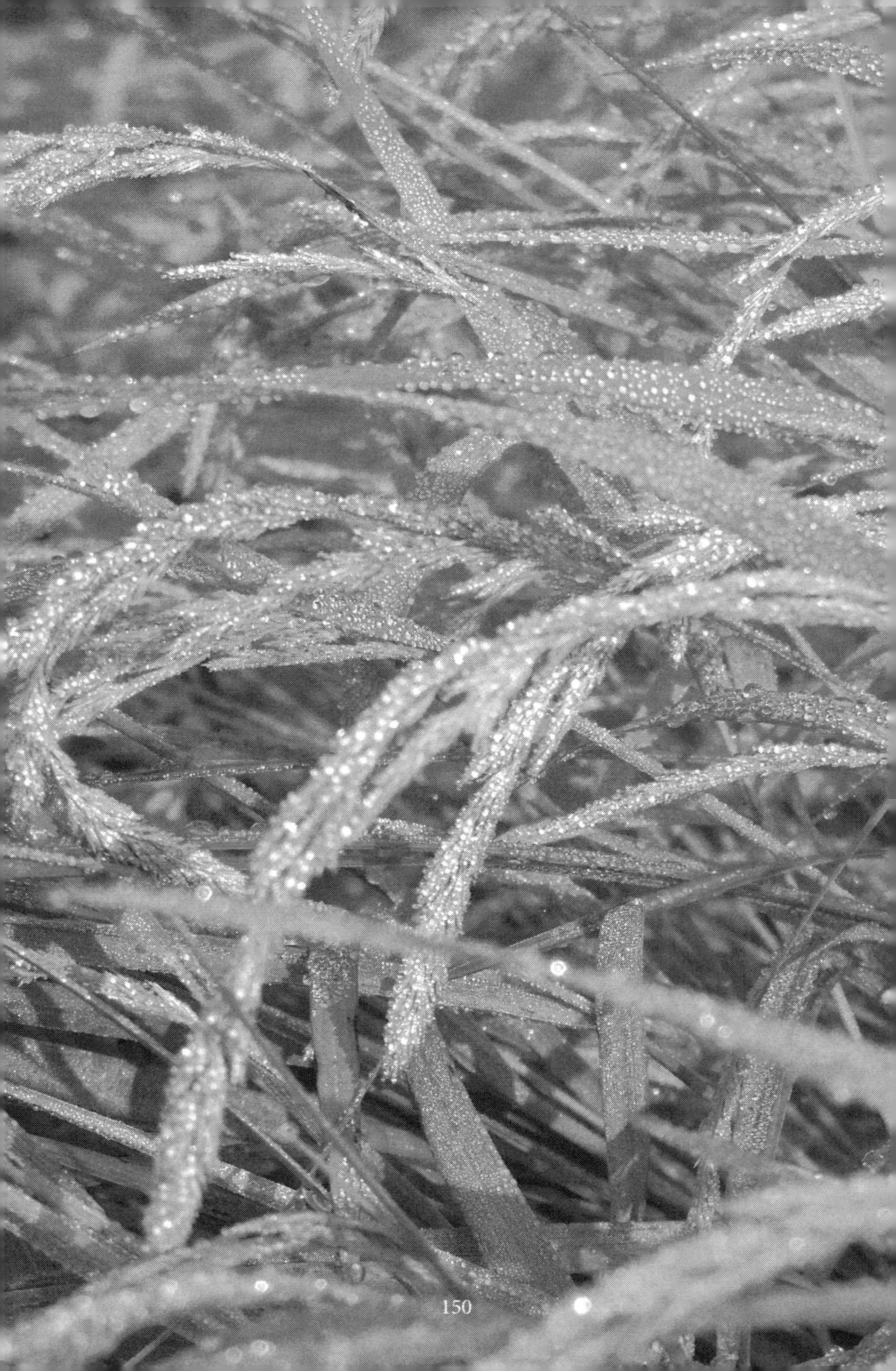

WEEK 37: FROM CONVICTION TO CONFESSION

CONSIDER:

Quack grass threatened to choke out my garden. Tenacious stuff! Herbicides "inhibit" it but don't kill it. Pulling the grass "inhibits" it but doesn't kill it. Black gardening fabric "inhibits" it but doesn't kill it. The only way to get rid of it for good is to dig out the thick white roots. So, year after year, I was elbow-deep in dirt, digging out the long underground runners. It was slow, painstaking work. By the time I finished a row, my hands were covered with small cuts and puncture wounds.

As I worked, God said, "You know, Michelle, conquering habitual sin is a lot like overcoming quack grass."

I thought it over during an ice water break. "You know, Lord, you're right," I replied. (Big surprise there, eh?)

Habitual sins can have a strong grip on us. Their roots run deep and must be destroyed so they won't choke out our spiritual fruit. But the task is slow and painful. We must choose holiness, time and time again. Choosing holiness means denying the flesh, time and time again. Finding strength for holy living means running to our Savior, time and time again. Dying to ourselves hurts!

If we continue to choose sin, we allow it to be our master — like quack grass running rampant in a garden. If we choose Christ, we allow Him to be master.

Do you not know that to whom you present yourselves slaves to obey, you are that one's slaves whom you obey, whether of sin leading to death, or of obedience leading to righteousness? (Romans 6:16)

When it feels like we're losing the battle, it helps to look back at sin issues God has already rooted out. Has God given you the strength to overcome an addiction? Are you less angry, impatient, or anxious? Have your priorities changed? Those old sin-bents may lurk at the edges of our hearts, waiting for an opportunity to encroach. But when we maintain a right stance before God, it keeps sin at bay.

The Holy Spirit *will* convict us of sin in our lives. It's not enough to acknowledge the conviction. We must confess the sin and turn from it. Only when we deny it a foothold will we see our spiritual fruit grow. Though our sins, like quack grass, won't be eradicated until Christ sets all thing right in heaven and on earth, let's keep working on rooting out evil.

DAY 1 | PRAY:

When I kept silent, my bones wasted away through my groaning all day long. For day and night your hand was heavy on me. My strength was sapped as in the heat of summer. Then I acknowledged my sin to you and did not cover up my iniquity, and you forgave the guilt of my sin. (Psalm 32)

DAY 2 | MEMORIZE:

2 Corinthians 7:9-10

Now I rejoice, not that you were made sorry, but that your sorrow led to repentance. For you were made sorry in a godly manner, that you might suffer loss from us in nothing. For godly sorrow produces repentance leading to salvation, not to be regretted; but the sorrow of the world produces death.

DAY 3 | READ AND RESPOND:

Ephesians 6:10-20

When we do battle with sin, who are we doing battle with?
_____
_____
_____

What tools has God given us to protect ourselves from Satan's attacks?
_____
_____
_____

What weapons has He given us to fight back and inflict wounds?
_____
_____
_____

Give an example of prayer's power in spiritual warfare from the Bible.
_____
_____
_____

DAY 4 | DO:

Find a tenacious weed growing in your yard. Try pulling it. Were you able to get the root out? What will happen if you pull the leaves but the root stays in the ground? Note any spiritual insights from this exercise.

REFLECTIONS

DAY 5 | JOURNAL:

Record prayers, thoughts, or insights from your time with God.

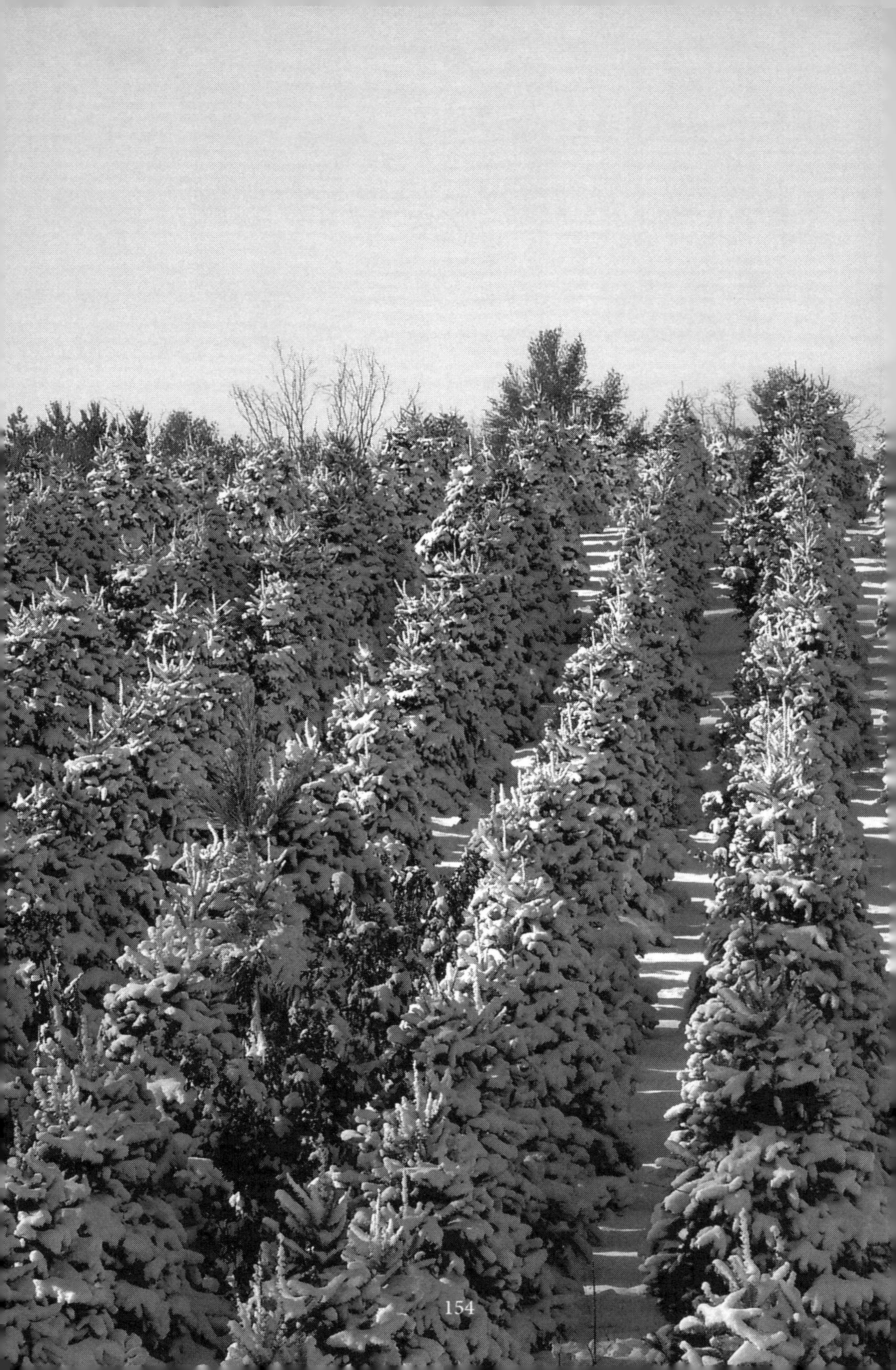

WEEK 38: FROM STRIVING TO ABIDING

CONSIDER:

My family and I tromped through powdery snow, searching the Christmas tree farm for the perfect evergreen. We found one — not too tall, too plump, or too scruffy. We settled on a balsam fir with sturdy branches for our heavier glass ornaments.

My husband laid on the ground, saw in hand, ready to begin cutting. "You're sure, now? This is the tree you want? Because once I start cutting, we're committed."

"Yes, we're sure." The conviction in our voices freed my husband to put the blade to the tree trunk and begin. It wasn't long before the tree toppled over. It looked beautiful sitting in the corner of our living room, decked out with bright lights, shining glass ornaments, and an angel topper. For a time.

We kept our Christmas tree watered but no matter how well we cared for it, the tree slowly died. The needles gradually dried up and fell off. Forever severed from its life-giving trunk, the tree could not survive. And there was no way to reunite tree and trunk, no way the tree could be revitalized.

We are born severed from God, fallen Christmas trees cut off from our life-giving trunk. Our sinful nature keeps us from being nurtured. We can strive to be good people. We can work hard to earn God's favor. Those around us may even be convinced we are true believers. After all, we look and talk and act like Christ-followers. But without first acknowledging our need for a Savior, our striving is in vain.

Unlike the Christmas tree, however, we don't have to remain cut off from our Trunk. We can be reunited, restored, and revitalized, grafted to the Living Vine.

That was the whole point of one tiny baby's birth. Christ humbled Himself and came to earth as a baby. He walked the earth as a child, died as a young man, and rose as a Savior — all so we could have an opportunity to find true life in His sacrifice for our sins.

When we humble ourselves and seek God's forgiveness, He heals the severing wound. As long as we abide in the vine, He nourishes us. We will never dry up, be unfruitful, or be separated from our life source again.

Learning to abide is a lifelong endeavor. It's so easy to fall back on our own strengths and talents or revert to doing things for our own glory rather than God's. We need to check our motives regularly. While we are still called to do good works (Philippians 2:12), we no longer need to win God's approval. We already have it! We can cease striving. (Psalm 46:10) Our faithful service can be an outpouring of Christ in us as we abide in Him.

> *I am the vine, you are the branches; he who abides in Me and I in him, he bears much fruit, for apart from Me you can do nothing.* (John 15:5)

DAY 1 | PRAY:

Lord, you are my refuge and my fortress, my God, in whom I trust. I will dwell in your shelter and rest in your shadow. Because you love me, Lord, you will rescue me. You will protect me, for I acknowledge your name. (Psalm 91)

DAY 2 | MEMORIZE:

1 John 2:28

And now, little children, abide in Him, that when He appears, we may have confidence and not be ashamed before Him at His coming.

READ AND RESPOND:

John 15:1-10

What happens when we are abiding in Christ, the vine?

_____
_____
_____

What does the vinedresser (God) do with unfruitful branches? With fruitful branches?

_____
_____
_____

Can we be fruitful apart from the vine? Which verse makes this clear?

_____
_____
_____

According to verse 8, why is abiding in the vine and bearing fruit important?

_____
_____
_____

DAY 4 | DO:

Buy some white daisies. Prepare several jars of water with different food dye colors. Put one or two daisies in each jar. What happens? All the daisies started out the same color. All are abiding in water. Do they all look the same after a few days drinking dyed water? What does this teach us about people abiding in Christ?

REFLECTIONS

DAY 5 | JOURNAL:

Record prayers, thoughts, or insights from your time with God.

(Photo credit: © [chungking] / Adobe Stock)

WEEK 39: FROM BUSY TO RESTFUL

CONSIDER:

A steady stream of little black soldiers marched one by one from tree to tree. The black ants wore a roadway into the grass, right under my clothesline.

Solomon instructed us, *"Go to the ant, o sluggard, observe her ways and be wise; which having no chief, officer or ruler, prepares her food in the summer and gathers her provision in the harvest."* (Proverbs 6:6-8)

So, as an act of obedience, I paused from my duties and watched the ants.

Their road was narrow, forcing them to move single file. The southbound ants carried food to their colony. The northbound ants were empty-handed. When they met the burdened ants, they greeted them with their antennae and then stepped aside.

The whole colony was preparing for the cold, cloistered underground months. Though they worked relentlessly at the time, their season of rest was coming. They bunkered below ground for the winter, relishing the fruits of their labor until favorable weather called them to the surface.

Finding the balance between work and rest, between busyness and laziness, is a lifelong struggle. Most of us have a bent toward either overworking or over-resting.

God has indeed given us work to do and declared it a blessing. Productivity is good for our minds and bodies and allows us to provide for ourselves.

Nothing is better for a man than that he should eat and drink, and that his soul should enjoy good in his labor. This also, I saw, was from the hand of God. (Ecclesiastes 2:24)

The Bible is quite clear we should work if we are able to. There should be no reward for someone who refuses to be productive.

For even when we were with you, we commanded you this: If anyone will not work, neither shall he eat. (2 Thessalonians 3:10)

God has also ordained rest. The Creator Himself rested from all His labors on the Sabbath — not because He was tired, but as an example to us. Leisure allows us to be still and know that He is God. (Psalm 46:10) It allows our minds, bodies, and spirits to recover from life's daily demands.

There remains therefore a rest for the people of God. For he who has entered His rest has himself also ceased from his works as God did from His. (Hebrews 4:9-10)

Our caring Father would have us find a wise balance, tackling the tasks He's given us and saying no to the tasks He hasn't so we have time to rest in Him.

DAY 1 | PRAY:

Lord, teach me to fear you and walk in your ways so I will enjoy your blessings. When I eat what the labor of my hands produces, I will be happy, and it will be well with me. Behold, you bless every person who fears you. (Psalm 128)

DAY 2 | MEMORIZE:

Colossians 3:17

And whatever you do in word or deed, do all in the name of the Lord Jesus, giving thanks to God the Father through Him.

DAY 3 | READ AND RESPOND:

Ecclesiastes 3:9-15

In verses 9-11, what does Solomon conclude about the work God has assigned us?

In verses 12-13, why does Solomon conclude we should enjoy our lives and our work?

Is there eternal value in the work we do? Why or why not?

Solomon hints at a mystery in verse 11. What is it? Why do you think it remains a mystery?

DAY 4 | DO:

Create or clip out a picture that represents where you work or would like to work. What about this work or work environment appeals to you? Create or clip out a picture of someplace you would find restful. What about this environment appeals to you? Ask God for opportunities to enjoy both.

DAY 5 | JOURNAL:

Record prayers, thoughts, or insights from your time with God.

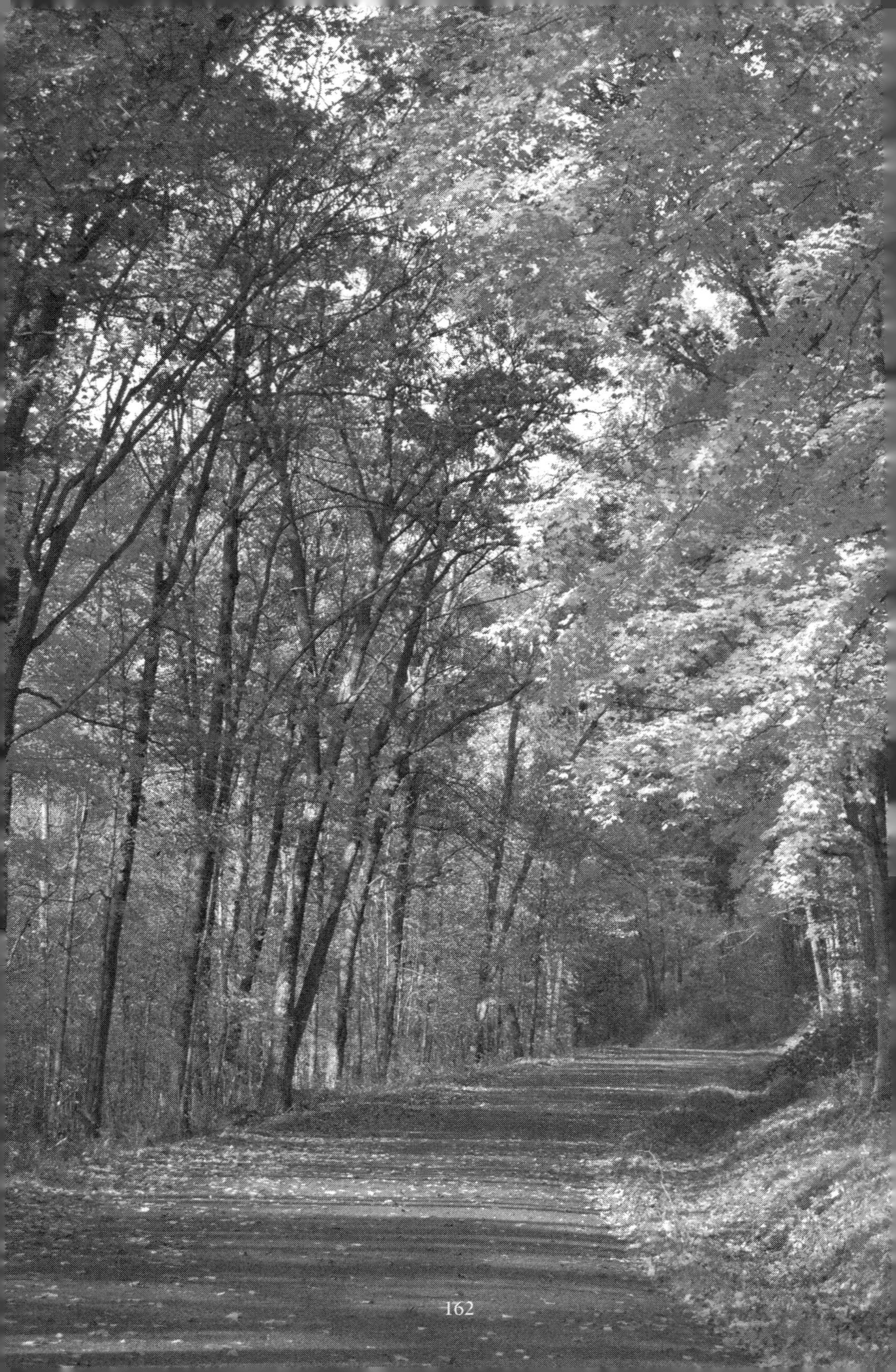

WEEK 40: FROM AIMLESS TO PURPOSEFUL

CONSIDER:

There's a beautiful county park just an hour from our house, along the banks of the Eau Pleine River. Mature hardwood forests and towering white pines create a canopy over the black-topped ribbon of a road leading to the park's center. In visits past, we've been to the beach, checked out the frisbee golf course, and chosen some premier sites we'd reserve if we had all the right camping gear.

When we last visited, we left home with no particular destination in mind and arrived at the park with no set plan. We decided to hike a woodland trail. Autumn-tinted leaves and acorns crunched underfoot as we ambled from marker to marker, learning about the varied tree species. Had we gotten bored or tired, we could have turned around. We were just enjoying a leisurely day together.

What a contrast to much of the hiking I've done. My hiking companions and I would set out with a trail map in hand and a specific destination in mind — usually a cabin or campsite where we were spending the night. There was no ambling. It was more like a death march! There was no turning back.

Apart from Christ, life is aimless. Oh, it's not that people can't (or don't) have goals and dreams. Many do. But we've all heard the stories of people who achieved everything they hoped for, only to realize the satisfaction they felt was temporal, at best. Many well-known, successful people have fallen into depression, addiction, or worse. Why? Even when there is eternal value in their accomplishments, they don't have the spiritual eyes to see it. They wander through life believing the ultimate destination is death. Nothing more. No hope beyond the grave.

> *But seek first the kingdom of God and His righteousness, and all these things shall be added to you.* (Matthew 6:33)

When Christ redeems us, He puts eternity in our hearts. He puts a trail map, His divinely inspired word, in our hands and sets us on the path to heaven. We have a set destination: our forever home in God's company. It gives meaning to our work, whatever our work may be. It influences how we invest our time, money, and talents. It gives our lives direction and purpose, even when we face hardships. It gives us hope in this world and beyond the grave. We're storing up treasures in heaven that will always satisfy. As the old hymn so aptly puts it, "We're marching to Zion." But unlike those hikes I took in my younger days, we're on a life march.

DAY 1 | PRAY:

Though I walk through troubled times, Lord, you preserve my life. You stretch out your hand against the wrath of my enemies and your right hand delivers me. You will fulfill your purpose for me; your steadfast love, O Lord, endures forever. Do not forsake the work of your hands. (Psalm 138)

DAY 2 | MEMORIZE:

Psalm 138:8 (ESV)

The Lord will fulfill his purpose for me; your steadfast love, O Lord, endures forever. Do not forsake the work of your hands.

DAY 3 | READ AND RESPOND:

2 Timothy 1:8-12

What purpose did God call Paul to? Was it an easy calling?

_____
_____
_____

What purpose has God called you to? What obstacles have you encountered while fulfilling it?

_____
_____
_____

Why was Paul not ashamed of joining in Christ's suffering?

_____
_____
_____

According to verse 12, what hope do you have as we obediently follow Christ?

_____
_____
_____

DAY 4 | DO:

Draw a picture of a simple object, perhaps a tree or a flower, with your eyes closed. Now draw the same picture with your eyes open. What difference does having your eyes open make in the outcome? If you are visually impaired, listen to a song with cotton balls in your ears. Now listen to the same song without anything in your ears. What difference does having your ears open make in the outcome?

DAY 5 | JOURNAL:

Record prayers, thoughts, or insights from your time with God.

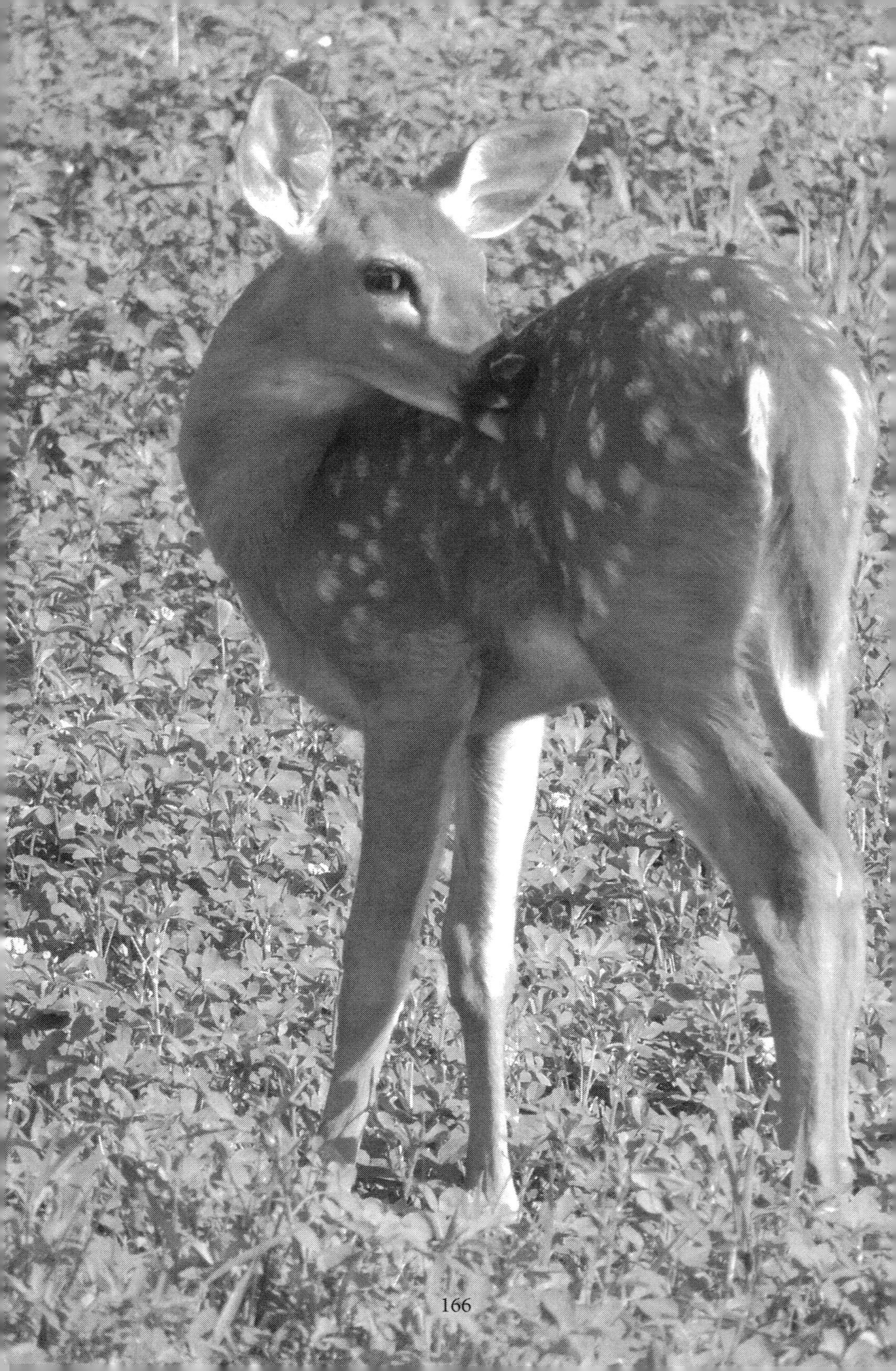

WEEK 41: FROM DOUBT TO SECURITY

CONSIDER:

I once saw two fawns playing in a puddle. I couldn't get out of my car without scaring the little ones, so I sat in the driver's seat, wishing I had my camera.

It began with one baby tentatively dipping a hoof in the cool water. He touched it, then jumped back. His sibling watched him circle around and make a fresh approach. This time, the fawn was bolder. He put one foot in until it, I presume, rested on solid ground. The water was up to his knee. Satisfied he wasn't stepping into a bottomless pit, he jumped in with abandon.

Curiosity got the better of the second fawn, who followed his bolder sibling into the pool. Before long, they were leaping and splashing and chasing each other through the water. They romped until they wore themselves out.

We approach new experiences much the same way. We're doubtful at first, unsure whether the harness we're strapped into on the high ropes course will catch us if we fall. We have to test it out, perhaps with some hesitation, to see whether it's secure.

We tend to approach our relationship with God in a similar fashion. We begin with doubts about whether He can be trusted. The Bible says He can be. But we must be convinced, through our own experiences, that it's true. So, we gingerly take a small step of faith and see what happens. Each time God proves Himself trustworthy, we proceed with less caution and more confidence.

When we doubt God and His word, we are vulnerable to Satan's attacks and false teachings.

For he who doubts is like a wave of the sea driven and tossed by the wind.
(James 1:6b)

God, through His unwavering care, removes all our reasons to doubt so we can securely rest in Him.

I will both lie down in peace, and sleep;
For You alone, O Lord, make me dwell in safety. (Psalm 4:8)

Can you imagine serving an unpredictable King? Think about being married to Henry VIII, the man who changed wives almost as often as he changed his undergarments. Their status was largely dependent on whether they could give the king a son. If they couldn't, he traded them in for a different model. They had no lasting security.

Praise God, He never changes! His unconditional love is unwavering. We can come boldly before His throne, in humble adoration, knowing He will always be eager to receive us.

DAY 1 | PRAY:

Almighty God, those who trust in you are like Mount Zion, which cannot be moved but abides forever. As the mountains surround Jerusalem, so you surround your people from this time forth and forever. Do good, O Lord, to those who are good, and upright in their hearts. (Psalm 125)

DAY 2 | MEMORIZE:

Psalm 16:8

*I have set the Lord always before me;
Because He is at my right hand I shall not be moved.*

DAY 3 | READ AND RESPOND:

John 20:24-31

Why do you think Thomas doubted Jesus had risen from the dead? Would you have doubted, too?

_____
_____
_____

How do we know, from this passage, God knows all our thoughts and doubts?

_____
_____
_____

How does Jesus respond to Thomas' doubts? How does He not respond?

_____
_____
_____

In verses 30 and 31, what reason does John give for recording stories from Jesus' life? How does his reasoning tie in with the last story he told?

_____
_____
_____

DAY 4 | DO:

If you have any doubts about God, write your concern(s) in your journal and date it. Ask God to alleviate your doubts. Recruit a trusted friend to pray with you. Continue praying until you find security where there was doubt. Record the date your prayer is answered.

REFLECTIONS

DAY 5 | JOURNAL:

Record prayers, thoughts, or insights from your time with God.

(Photo credit © (goluboyj) / Adobe Stock)

WEEK 42: FROM DUTY TO CALLING

CONSIDER:

Don Shire is a talented trumpeter. His ministry goes beyond encouraging believers through his musical abilities to inviting others to help meet the needs of widows, orphans, and the homeless.

I once heard Mr. Shire say, "Some people play notes, others play music."

I observed this when I taught piano lessons but could never put words to it. Some of my students had solid technical ability. They played the correct notes and rhythms. They had good posture and technique. But they lacked heart or emotion. The music didn't touch them at all. They played notes.

Some of my students, on the other hand, connected with the music. Their technical skills melded with their very being. When they played, they poured a part of themselves into the notes and rhythms. They played music.

The Bible instructs us to be and to do many things. It is our God-given responsibility to join Him in His kingdom work here on earth.

The end of the matter; all has been heard. Fear God and keep his commandments, for this is the whole duty of man. (Ecclesiastes 12:13, ESV)

The question is, are we going to play notes or are we going to play music? It comes down to our hearts. What is our motivation for serving God and keeping His commandments?

Serving God and others out of duty or obligation is like playing the notes. We go through the motions and get the job done, but there's no joy in it. We may even do it for the feel-good praise and attention we get from others, receiving our reward here on earth. There's a disconnect between our hands and our hearts. People will still be blessed by our service. God will still be honored by our obedience. But when He looks at our motives, He won't see the stuff eternal rewards are made of.

"For the Lord does not see as man sees; for man looks at the outward appearance, but the Lord looks at the heart." (1 Samuel 16:7b)

When we see our kingdom work as a divine calling, however, we make music. Our service for God and others comes from the overflow of our hearts. Blessing others and honoring God are more than an outcome of our work. They are the motivation behind it. We can be content even when our work goes unnoticed for the sheer joy of investing in eternity.

DAY 1 | PRAY:

Lord, you saved me and called me to a holy life — not because of anything I have done but because of your own purpose and grace. Search me, O God, and know my heart. Try me, and know my anxieties. See if there is any wicked way in me and lead me in your everlasting way. (2 Timothy 1, Psalm 139)

DAY 2 | MEMORIZE:

Colossians 3:1-3

If then you were raised with Christ, seek those things which are above, where Christ is, sitting at the right hand of God. Set your mind on things above, not on things on the earth. For you died, and your life is hidden with Christ in God.

DAY 3 | READ AND RESPOND:

1 Corinthians 3:9-15

Do we work for God or with God? Why does the distinction matter?

_____
_____
_____

What foundation should we be building on? What if we don't build on it?

_____
_____
_____

How will God test our works to see which will endure as eternal rewards?

_____
_____
_____

What do we (and don't we) lose if our works don't survive the test?

_____
_____
_____

DAY 4 | DO:

Start a small fire (someplace safe) with paper, kindling, and wood. Once it's burning, throw an aluminum can or two in it. What changes do you see in the items being burned? Does anything survive the fire? Note any spiritual insights God gave you.

REFLECTIONS

DAY 5 | JOURNAL:

Record prayers, thoughts, or insights from your time with God.

CHICKADEES

All is still. Even the wind.
I stop to silence Styrofoam snow underfoot.
                        I listen to stillness.

At first there is nothing.
The only voice is color.
      Blaze blue sky.
            Grave gray maple.
                  Winter white birch.
                        Glossy green pine.
                              Lamb's wool snow.

Now a new voice. High, almost unheard.
Another the same.
      Chickadees.
Small winter wonders singing in flight.
      Joy and jubilation.
Celebration of God's provision in seasons
      Of hardship.

WEEK 43: FROM WORRY TO CONFIDENCE

CONSIDER:

Chickadees flit from tree to tree outside our window. They fluff their feathers against winter's bitter cold and go about their search for food, carefree and confident their Maker will provide for their needs. Though they are small and vulnerable, they are undaunted by the natural enemies threatening to claim their fragile lives: cold, starvation, or a hungry hawk.

God brings Abraham and Isaac to mind. Father and son are climbing Mt. Moriah to make sacrifices to Yahweh. Isaac, fully trusting his father, carries on carefree. Abraham, trusting in his Father, carries on confident God will make good on His promise to make him the father of a great nation. As they approach the top of the mountain, Isaac asks his dad, "Aren't you forgetting something?"

"I don't think so," Abraham answers.

"So, where's the lamb, Dad?"

"God will provide, son. God will provide."

And He did. That was the first time Yahweh was called Jehovah-Jireh, "the Lord will see it: He will provide."

I suppose if we had pea-sized brains and good instincts, like those chickadees, we wouldn't worry either. If you're like me, it would be a welcome relief to be freed from the complexities of human life. We know God tells us to cast our burdens on Him, but frankly, "let go and let God" is easier said than done. Learning not to worry takes practice; practice shutting down the frantic thoughts, taking our concerns to God in prayer, then resting in His promises to care for us.

Worry is a symptom. It's an indicator our trust in God is iffy. Yes, we believe in God's goodness, sovereignty, and ability to provide for our needs — on an intellectual level, anyway. But do we live by faith in those truths? We have no reason not to but sometimes it's difficult. Each time we find the strength to give our cares to Jehovah-Jireh, He proves Himself faithful. The longer we walk with God, trusting Him to care for us rather than wringing our hands with worry, the more confident we become in God's faithfulness. Our flesh and spirit wrestle less and rest more.

Be anxious for nothing, but in everything by prayer and supplication, with thanksgiving, let your requests be made known to God; and the peace of God, which surpasses all understanding, will guard your hearts and minds through Christ Jesus. (Philippians 4:6-7)

DAY 1 | PRAY:

The eyes of all look to you, Lord, and you give them their food in due season. You open your hand and satisfy the desire of every living thing. You satisfy the longing soul and fill the hungry soul with good things. You are righteous in all your ways and kind in all your works. (Psalm 145, Psalm 107)

DAY 2 | MEMORIZE:

Matthew 6:26

Look at the birds of the air, for they neither sow nor reap nor gather into barns; yet your heavenly Father feeds them. Are you not of more value than they?

DAY 3 | READ AND RESPOND:

Genesis 21:1-20

Why did Sarah want Hagar and Ishmael sent away?
_____
_____
_____

How did Abraham feel about sending them into the wilderness?
_____
_____
_____

What did Hagar do when she ran out of food and water?
_____
_____
_____

Did God provide for Hagar's needs? Why?
_____
_____
_____

DAY 4 | DO:

Set aside half an hour this week to watch some birds, any kind of birds. If you're artistic, maybe you'd like to draw a picture of the birds you observe. What lessons, if any, did you learn from watching them?

REFLECTIONS

DAY 5 | JOURNAL:

Record prayers, thoughts, or insights from your time with God.

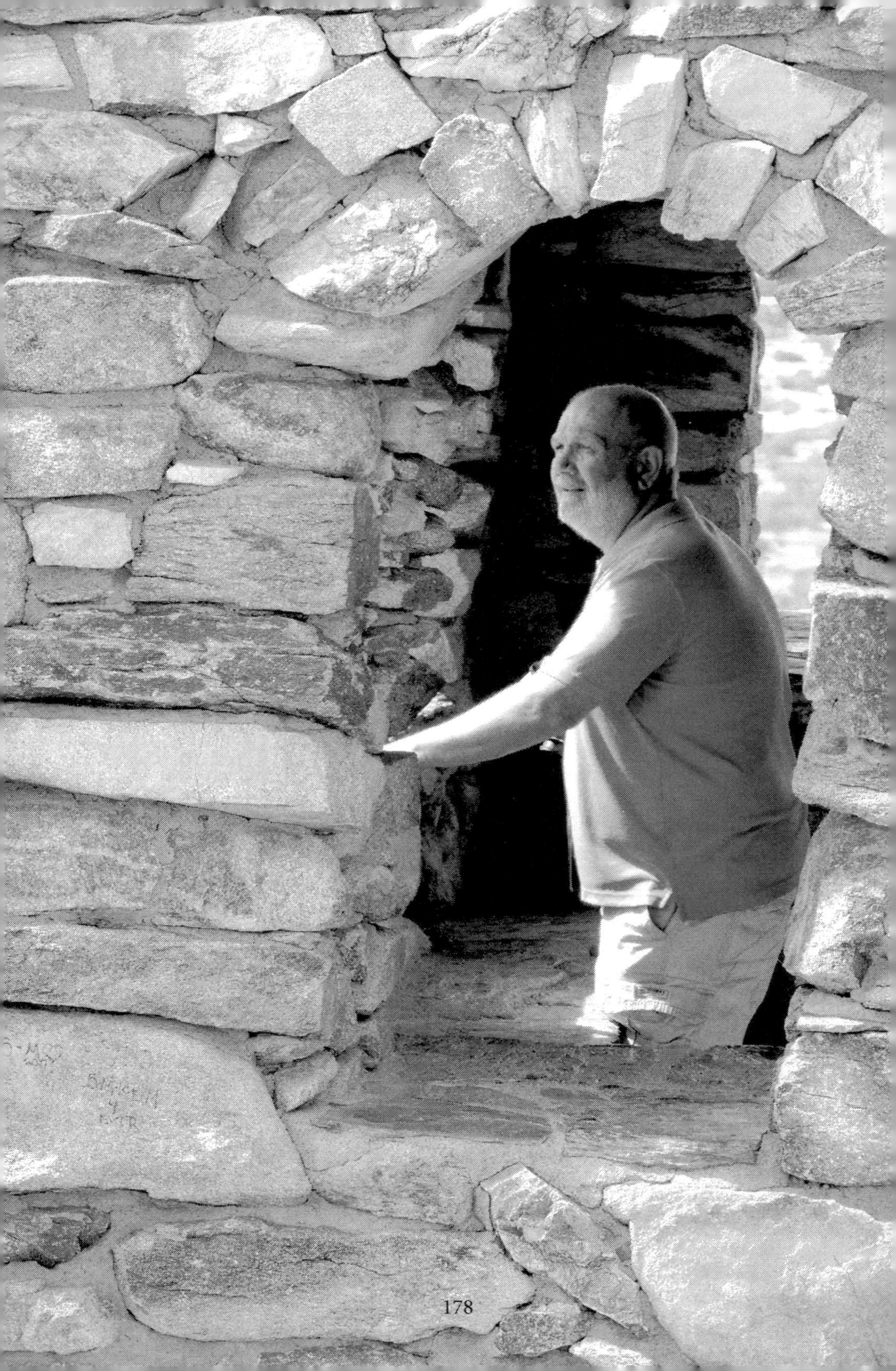

WEEK 44: FROM UNCERTAINTY TO FAITH

CONSIDER:

I was still single when I was 33. People tend to marry later in life these days, but I'm a boomer. In my generation, women who weren't married by their mid-20s were anomalies, pariahs cast out as "old maids" like the unpopped popcorn kernels that shared the unbecoming label.

I finally had a frank conversation about my singlehood with God. "Here's the thing, Lord. I could be content being single. But if I'm gonna get married, I'd like to know. Could you fill me in on the secret, please?" While waiting for God's answer on the marriage issue, I pursued mission opportunities in Africa. It felt like God would never answer my prayer, as the application process dragged on. God wasn't opening doors for me to serve overseas, nor was He sending eligible young men my way. The uncertainty of my future hovered like a low-hanging cloud bank just out of reach. I continued praying and clung to this promise:

And the Lord, He is the One who goes before you. He will be with you, He will not leave you nor forsake you; do not fear nor be dismayed. (Deuteronomy 31:8)

And then it happened, out of the blue. Someone introduced me to my husband, Peter. As we shook hands, I clearly heard the voice of the Spirit say, in my head, "This is the man you're going to marry." I answered, "Okay," (in my head) and just like that, it was settled. All I had to do was rest in God and wait, in faith, for Him to fulfill His promise.

We face many uncertainties in our lives. Some leave us fearful or dismayed. A dear friend's husband was just diagnosed with Stage 4 cancer. She wrestles with questions about what the future holds, struggling with the uncertainties of life without the man she loves by her side. She continually takes her questions and cares to God. Little by little, He is replacing her uncertainties with faith as she rests more and more in His promise.

Whatever our circumstances, God goes before us. He knows what the future holds. He will be with us as we walk into the unknown, and He will stay with us throughout our journey. When the path ahead is hidden, we can face uncertainties without fear or discouragement — by faith.

For we walk by faith, not by sight. (2 Corinthians 5:7)

DAY 1 | PRAY:

Faith is the assurance of things hoped for, the conviction of things not seen. I walk by faith, not by sight. So, I will trust in you, Lord, with all my heart and not lean on my own understanding. In all my ways, I will acknowledge you, and you will direct my paths. (Hebrews 11, Proverbs 3)

DAY 2 | MEMORIZE:

1 John 5:4 (NIV)

For everyone born of God overcomes the world. This is the victory that has overcome the world, even our faith.

DAY 3 | READ AND RESPOND:

Joshua 2:1-21

What did Rahab do to help the spies sent by the Israelites?

_____
_____
_____

What did she ask of the spies in return?

_____
_____
_____

Did the spies keep their promise? See Joshua 6:22-25.

_____
_____
_____

How do we know God redeemed Rahab's past and blessed her faith? See James 2:25 and Matthew 1:5.

_____
_____
_____

DAY 4 | DO:

Turn your faucet on. What did you expect to happen and why? (You can turn the faucet off now if you haven't already). If you had an unexpected outcome (i.e., nothing happened), what would that indicate? What would you do next? Consider the parallels between this exercise and faith.

REFLECTIONS

DAY 5 | JOURNAL:

Record prayers, thoughts, or insights from your time with God.

(photo credit © [Sonja E.] / Adobe Stock)

WEEK 45: FROM FAITHLESS TO FAITHFUL

CONSIDER:

Some years ago, we picked up a 5-year-old dog at a rummage sale. Her owner was moving into an apartment and couldn't take her along, so Cuddles needed a new home. The black, mini cocker spaniel's life experience, to that point, was watching TV with her owner and eating candy. Oh, and being "teased" by her grandson.

Cuddles had trust issues. For months, every time a man reached down to pet her, she cowered and left a puddle on the floor. And if you approached her while she was chewing on a bone or eating, she growled and snapped. The only person she had faith in was the woman who loved her first. Life at our house was a big adjustment, but things slowly changed for the better.

Over time, Cuddles learned we had her best interests at heart. She looked forward to walks that had exhausted her the first few months. She came to understand a hand reaching down carried a gentle stroke rather than a harsh rebuke. Because of her newfound trust, she quit cowering, growling, and snapping. She developed unwavering faith in us and was our faithful companion for eight years.

We must have faith to even begin communing with God.

For everyone born of God overcomes the world. This is the victory that has overcome the world, even our faith. Who is it that overcomes the world? Only the one who believes that Jesus is the Son of God. (1 John 5:4-5, NIV)

But greater faith is also cultivated over time. We take some tentative steps in our early days, uncertain whether God can always be trusted. Perhaps our life experiences undermined our ability to believe He has our best interests at heart. But each time He reaches down with a gentle touch — meeting our needs, healing our wounds, guiding us along the way — our faith grows. God's unchanging nature gives us confidence to trust Him in all things. In response, we become faithful followers, loyal servants and true companions of our Lord and King.

Our faith and our faithfulness please God, probably beyond our comprehension. Not only is it impossible to find God's favor without faith, He waits to heap blessings on those who chase hard after Him.

But without faith it is impossible to please Him, for he who comes to God must believe that He is, and that He is a rewarder of those who diligently seek Him. (Hebrews 11:6)

DAY 1 | PRAY:

Lord, I long to hear you say, "Well done, good and faithful servant! Come and share your master's happiness!" So, I will fear you, Lord, and serve you faithfully with all my heart, for you have done great things for me. (Matthew 25, 1 Samuel 12)

DAY 2 | MEMORIZE:

Luke 17:5

And the apostles said to the Lord, "Increase our faith."

DAY 3 | READ AND RESPOND:

James 1:2-8

How does God test our faith?

_____
_____
_____

Why does God test our faith?

_____
_____
_____

What role does wisdom play in our faith?

_____
_____
_____

How can doubt undermine our faith? Does this mean we should never question what we believe?

_____
_____
_____

DAY 4 | DO:

Find a foot bridge in your area. Take time to walk across it. Pause in the middle and consider faith. Are you exercising faith in the bridge? What, if anything, would make you question whether the bridge could be trusted? Record anything God brings to mind about faith and faithfulness.

REFLECTIONS

DAY 5 | JOURNAL:

Record prayers, thoughts, or insights from your time with God.

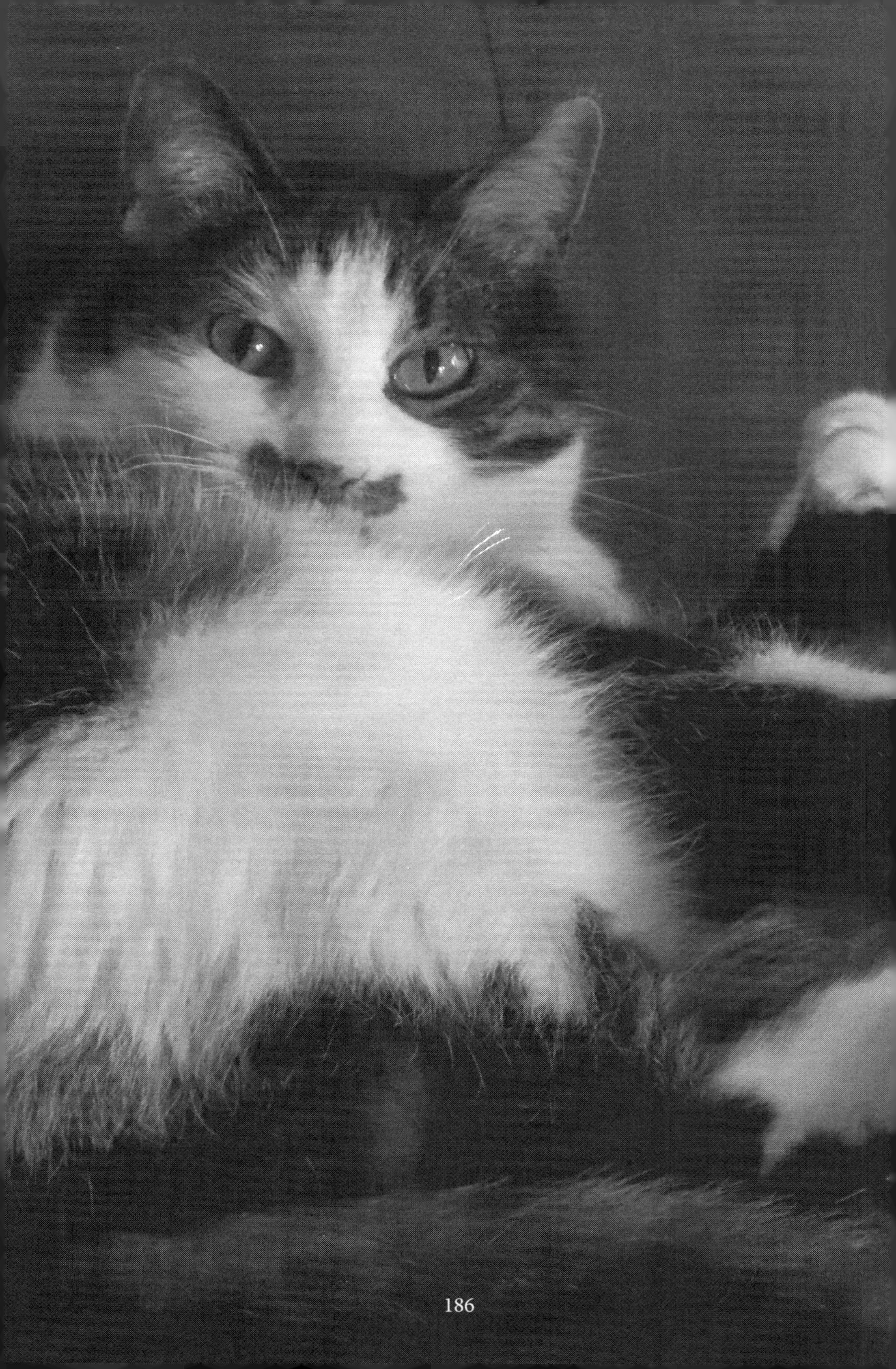

WEEK 46: FROM WANT TO PLENTY

CONSIDER:

A few years ago, a stray cat took up residence in our barn. She wasn't a feral cat. She came when we called her and rubbed against our legs. Her thin frame begged for food. She purred loudly as we pet her and scratched her scrawny chin. The girls and I made a cozy basket-bed for her, complete with a heating pad, in the milk house. We fed her and loved on her. We made sure she had everything she needed. She fattened up in no time. Then she fattened up even more. She was pregnant.

Before long, we had five cats sleeping in the basket-bed. It was great fun watching the little ones grow from helpless, hesitant creatures to curious, rambunctious kittens. Thankfully, we found good homes for them all. We also made sure our adoptee would never bless us with another bundle of kittens.

We come to Christ like our barn cat came to us: hungry, lacking a safe place to rest, and longing for care and kindness. Some of us are even dumped off, rejected by someone who was supposed to care for us. When we run to Jesus, He adopts us. He gives us living water and the bread of eternal life. He showers us with compassion and gives us a safe place to rest.

> *He who dwells in the secret place of the Most High*
> *Shall abide under the shadow of the Almighty.*
> *I will say of the Lord, "He is my refuge and my fortress;*
> *My God, in Him I will trust.* (Psalm 91:1-2)

That's not to say we'll never have unmet physical or financial needs again. The apostle Paul, even when he was faithfully following God, knew what it was to have plenty and nothing, to be well-fed and hungry (Philippians 4). Evil will hound us even more when we're determined to walk with God.

But in Christ, we will always have plenty, in spiritual terms. God will give us strength when our human weakness tries to undermine us. He will guide us when the way ahead is obscured. He will invite us to rest when we are weary. He will feed our souls until the day He calls us home and we leave our want behind forever.

> *And God is able to make all grace abound toward you, that you, always having all sufficiency in all things, may have an abundance for every good work.*
> (2 Corinthians 9:8)

DAY 1 | PRAY:

Many, Lord my God, are the wonders you have done, the things you planned for me. None can compare with you. If I were to talk about all your deeds, they would be too many to declare. (Psalm 40)

DAY 2 | MEMORIZE:

Psalm 34:9

Oh, fear the Lord, you His saints!
There is no want to those who fear Him.

DAY 3 | READ AND RESPOND:

1 Kings 17:1-9

Why does Elijah need special provision from God in this story?

How did Elijah respond to God's direction? Did he follow God with confidence or doubt? Defend your answer.

How did God provide Elijah's food and water, despite the drought in the land?

What happened when the stream dried up? Was Elijah left to die?

DAY 4 | DO:

Think of a time when you were in want of something crucial. How did God meet your need? Did He give you just enough or more than enough? What, if anything, did you learn from the experience?

REFLECTIONS

DAY 5 | JOURNAL:

Record prayers, thoughts, or insights from your time with God.

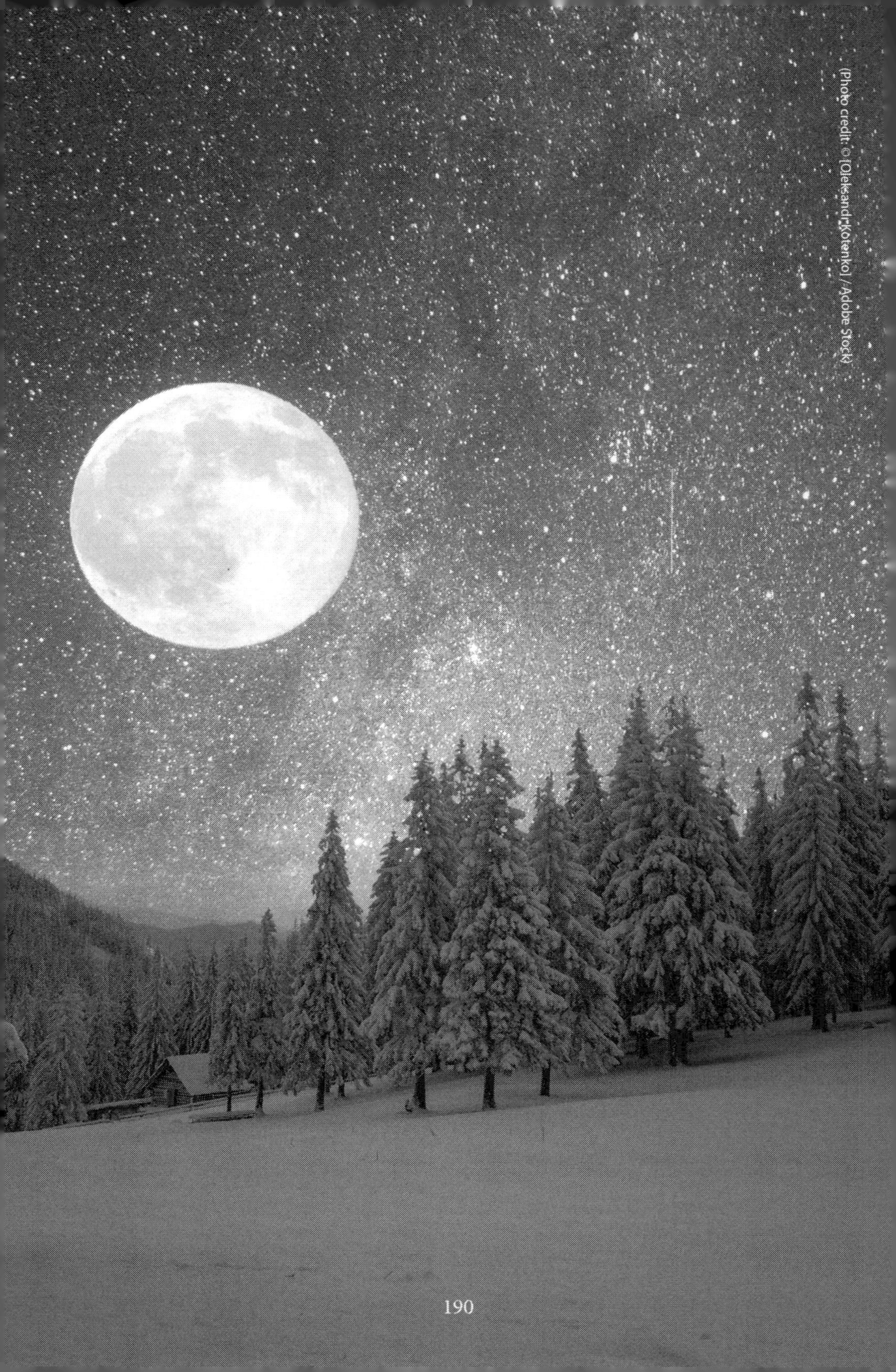
(Photo credit: © [Oleksandr Kotenko] / Adobe Stock)

WEEK 47: FROM COMPLAINING TO CONTENTMENT

CONSIDER:

A cold moon cast bold shadows over the crisp snow. Venus hovered in the night sky, outshining all her co-stars. And the Big Dipper hung low on the horizon, slopping all its contents over the down-turned handle and onto the treetops. Underfoot, the snow creaked a complaint about the weight of my boots. We both wished it was just a little warmer. I chuckled at the thought.

Why am I prone to be discontent? When it's hot and humid, I wish it was cooler. When it's cold and snowy, I long for summer days. I complain when it rains if I planned to bike. I complain if the sun warms the snow if I planned to ski. Complain, complain, complain.

I recently heard a preacher say complaining is rooted in selfishness. Ouch! When I look at my trivial complaints, I know it's true. My grumbling is rooted in the gap between my expectations and my reality. The Father often checks my heart through the words and insights of fellow believers, then brings me back to the truths in His word. In Philippians, the apostle Paul told his church family:

Do all things without grumbling or disputing. (Philippians 2:14)

We aren't instructed to do what we do heartily (Colossians 3:23) just for our own morale — though a cheerful outlook goes a long way toward finding contentment. Though it isn't always evident right away, trials come with blessings. Focusing on the good God is doing helps us make peace with the unsavory aspects of our daily grind. As Mary Poppins put it, "Just a spoonful of sugar helps the medicine go down."

There are bigger reasons to carry out our duties without complaining. It honors God, of course. But it also opens doors. Paul went on to say:

That you may become blameless and harmless, children of God without fault in the midst of a crooked and perverse generation, among whom you shine as lights in the world. (Philippians 2:15)

Not complaining is a countercultural concept. If we can learn to be content in any circumstance, if we can accomplish our work without grumbling, if we serve without butting heads with those around us, we will be a light in the darkness, a shining ambassador for Christ, a daily testament to God's faithfulness. People will notice our contentment and be drawn to the Author of it. By God's incomparable strength, we can live above the fray.

For I have learned in whatever state I am, to be content. (Philippians 4:11b)

WEEK 47

DAY 1 | PRAY:

Lord, in regard to need, teach me in whatever situation I find myself, to be content, whether I am in dire need or abundantly blessed. Everywhere and in all things, I must learn to be content, whether full or hungry, whether abounding in your provision or suffering need. I can do all things through you, because you strengthen me. (Philippians 4)

DAY 2 | MEMORIZE:

1 Timothy 6:6

Now godliness with contentment is great gain.

DAY 3 | READ AND RESPOND:

Leviticus 11:1-9

What were the Israelites complaining about?

_____
_____
_____

Why were they discontent with the food God miraculously sent from heaven?

_____
_____
_____

How did God respond to their complaining?

_____
_____
_____

God doesn't rain down fire when we complain. But what can we learn from this story?

_____
_____
_____

DAY 4 | DO:

Think about when you are most content. For me, it's when I'm snuggling under a warm blanket with my husband. Seek out your special contentment situation at least once a week. Bring it to mind when you're tempted to complain.

REFLECTIONS

DAY 5 | JOURNAL:

Record prayers, thoughts, or insights from your time with God.

194

WEEK 48: FROM TEMPORAL TO ETERNAL

CONSIDER:

One day, I looked out the window and saw our resident red squirrel raiding the apple tree. She leapt along to the end of a branch much too thin to hold her lightweight frame. The branch bent nearly to the ground, burdened not only by the apples it bore but by the added weight of a hungry squirrel. She bit into a little green apple and tugged until the stem let loose. Then she scampered down the squat tree trunk, across the lawn, and up to the lowest limb of our red pine.

The apple she carried was nearly as big as her. Yet, she was determined to take it home. Suddenly, Ginger (that's what the girls named her) realized I was spying on her. She scurried up the tree and took a flying leap to the nearby birch. I lost her in the branches and filtered sunlight. She reappeared moments later, apple-less. She had stowed her treasure safely away and returned to chew me out. She hung upside down from a limb, chattering and chirping. With each rebuke, she flicked her furry tail, as if punctuating her message with an exclamation mark.

We can fall into the trap of laying up and guarding earthly treasures like Ginger gathered and guarded her apples. It's not wrong to have nice things, but the truth is many of us have more nice things than we can use or enjoy. We rent storage units to house our excess possessions. Trust me. I'm not pointing fingers. We live on a farm. Our barn, machine shed, granary, and two-car garage are stuffed with stuff my husband and I are storing.

None of it really belongs to us. When we leave this temporal world, someone will divide and sell off the spoils while God weighs out our heavenly treasures. When He throws a lifetime of spent money, time, and energy on His purifying fire, how much wood, hay, and stubble will burn away? How much gold, silver, and precious stone will survive?

> *Now if anyone builds on this foundation with gold, silver, precious stones, wood, hay, straw, each one's work will become clear; for the Day will declare it, because it will be revealed by fire; and the fire will test each one's work, of what sort it is.*
> (1 Corinthians 3:12-13)

Since we are no longer of this world, our prizes and priorities are no longer worldly things. God recruited us to help with His eternal work. Storing up eternal treasures in heaven — investing our time, talents, and finances as God leads us — brings us greater joy and God greater glory.

> *But seek first the kingdom of God and His righteousness, and all these things shall be added to you.* (Matthew 6:33)

DAY 1 | PRAY:

Lord, before the mountains were created, or you had formed the earth and the world, from everlasting to everlasting, you are God. To you, a thousand years are like yesterday when it is past. So, teach me to number my days that I may have a heart of wisdom. (Psalm 90)

DAY 2 | MEMORIZE:

Matthew 6:19-21

Do not lay up for yourselves treasures on earth, where moth and rust destroy and where thieves break in and steal; but lay up for yourselves treasures in heaven, where neither moth nor rust destroys and where thieves do not break in and steal. For where your treasure is, there your heart will be also.

DAY 3 | READ AND RESPOND:

Luke 12:13-21

Why does Jesus warn us to beware of covetousness? What does it lead to?

What did the rich man hope to accomplish? Was he successful?

What can we learn from the rich man's mistakes?

What is Jesus' final observation in this parable?

DAY 4 | DO:

Eliminate one purchase a week. It could be a meal out, a coffee shop beverage, an Amazon order, or something you don't really need at the store. Note when you start and put away the money you saved for one year. Put away cash so you see it grow and don't spend it. At the end of the year, lay up a heavenly treasure. Donate the money to your church or a ministry. Or buy something your local food pantry or shelter needs and drop it off. Whether your gift is large or small, it will be a blessing.

REFLECTIONS

DAY 5 | JOURNAL:

Record prayers, thoughts, or insights from your time with God.

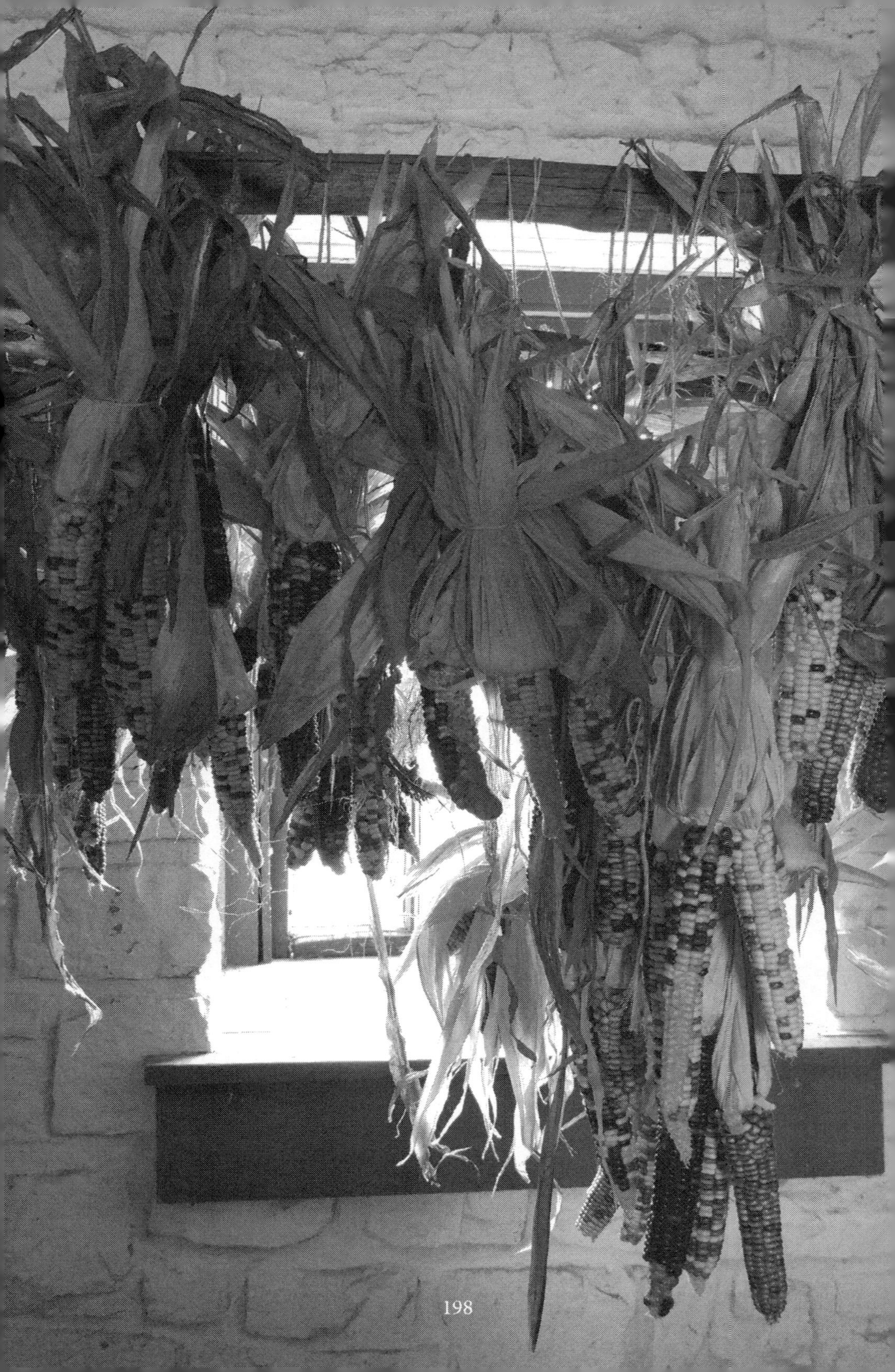

WEEK 49: FROM YOUTH TO OLD AGE

CONSIDER:

The temperature said summer but the aroma said autumn. Though it was unseasonably warm, the air was fall scent infused. I soaked in the sweet, musty smell of fading flowers mingled with sun-drenched leaves and pine windfall baking in the hot sun.

My garden said it was autumn, too. I harvested and preserved more so I gave more away. My string beans were finally strung out. My cucumber vines were in a pickle. And my sweet corn was earless. Only my cold-weather veggies were still cranking out crops.

My body also agreed it was fall. It would be an overstatement to say I felt old, but I certainly didn't feel young anymore. And I feel the slow drift toward winter a bit more each year. My energy level is falling with the leaves. My memory is decaying with the windfall. And my body is fading with the flowers. My only hope is in knowing God has preserved my soul.

Our culture sees getting older as some kind of cruel curse but aging is an honorable thing in Scripture. Younger people are instructed to treat older folks with dignity and deference, and for good reasons (1 Timothy 5:1-2). With age comes the wisdom of experience.

Wisdom is with aged men,
And with length of days, understanding. (Job 12:12)

The gray hair represents a life devoted to righteous living.

The silver-haired head is a crown of glory,
If it is found in the way of righteousness. (Proverbs 16:31)

And the life devoted to Christ never ceases to lose its purpose.

Those who are planted in the house of the Lord
Shall flourish in the courts of our God.
They shall still bear fruit in old age;
They shall be fresh and flourishing. (Psalm 92:13-14)

God has ordained aging as a natural aspect of our lives. Most of us find our troubles and sorrows increase with age, still we can enjoy the fruits of our years of labor and the autumn aroma of security in Christ. Each season brings us closer to our true home. Death ushers us into perfect fellowship with our Savior. What do we have to fear?

The days of our lives are seventy years;
And if by reason of strength they are eighty years,
Yet their boast is only labor and sorrow;
For it is soon cut off, and we fly away. (Psalm 90:10)

DAY 1 | PRAY:

Since my youth, God, you have taught me, and to this day I declare your marvelous deeds. Even when I am old and gray, do not forsake me, my God, till I declare your power to the next generation, your mighty acts to all who are to come. (Psalm 71)

DAY 2 | MEMORIZE:

2 Corinthians 4:16

Therefore we do not lose heart. Even though our outward man is perishing, yet the inward man is being renewed day by day.

DAY 3 | READ AND RESPOND:

Titus 2:1-8

According to this passage, how should older men behave?

How should older women act?

This passage explains how older men and women can be fruitful. What are they to do?

Why is it important for the older generation to obey and honor God?

DAY 4 | DO:

**The passage in Titus provides a model for discipleship.
If you are a younger person, pray for and seek out a spiritual mentor.
If you are an older person, pray about who God would want you to disciple.**

REFLECTIONS

DAY 5 | JOURNAL:

Record prayers, thoughts, or insights from your time with God.

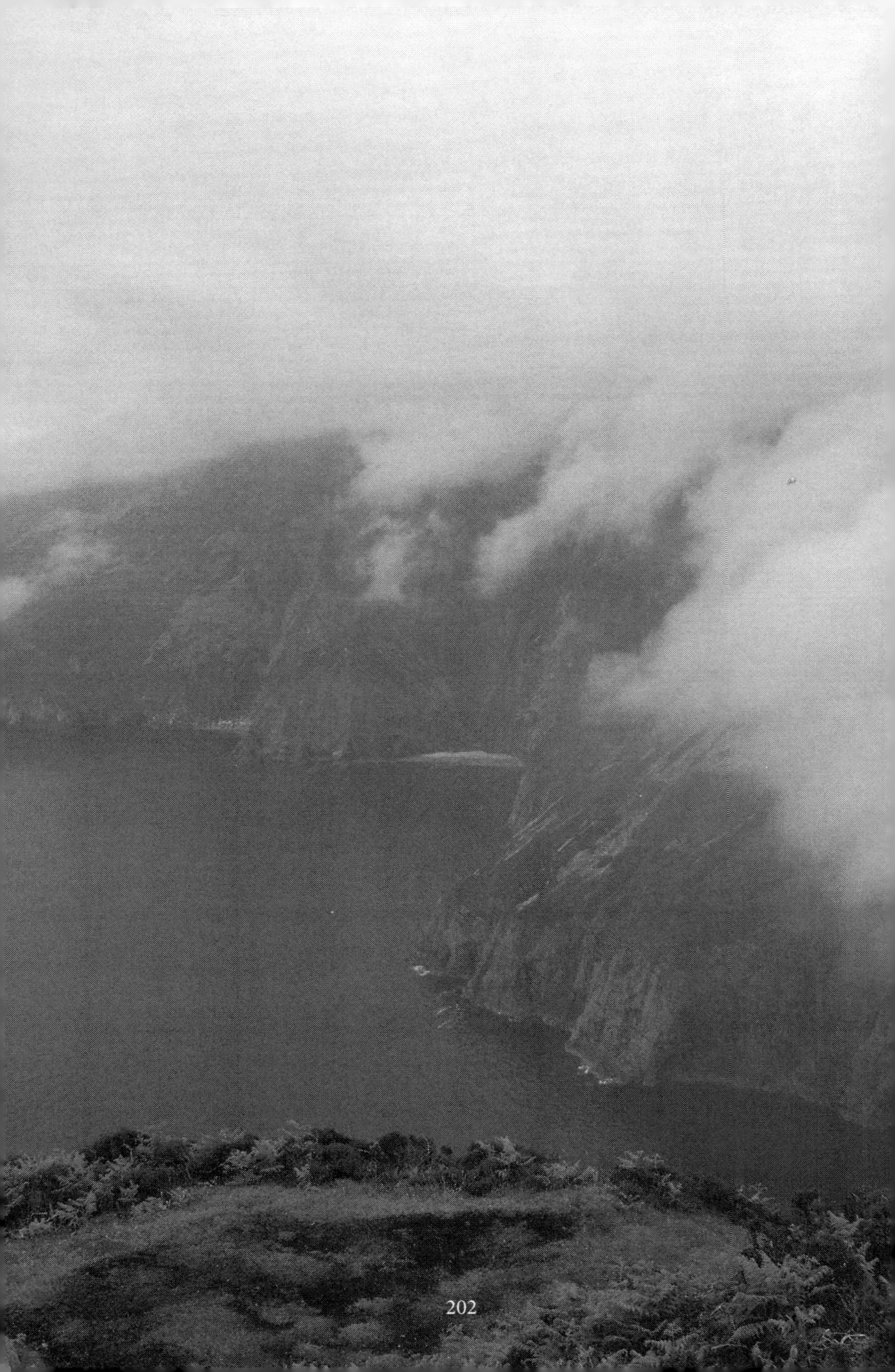

WEEK 50: FROM MOURNING TO REJOICING

CONSIDER:

A dismal, gray sky spilled light drizzle, casting a mournful mood over the landscape. It brought to mind the people I've loved well and lost — friends and family God called from this life to the next. I shed a few silent tears while driving the narrow road lined with leafless, lifeless-looking trees.

Then a little chuckle broke through the tears. I remembered the day I was mindlessly munching away at a pile of those tempting foil-wrapped chocolates on the table in front of me. I was reaching for number four (or was it number five?) when an arm quietly reached in front of me and swept the temptation out of reach. I glanced over at my dear friend, who had a knowing grin on his face and a newly acquired pile of candy. I leaned over and whispered, "Thank you!"

Taking chocolate from a chocoholic was a somewhat risky thing to do. He really was a true friend... a rare find, to be sure. My friend is now absent from the body and present with the Lord, which is far better — for him. But some days I still feel the sting, even though I know we will one day be reunited.

The absence of loved ones does not always seem "far better," at least not for us. Though we are thankful those who died in Christ are no longer enduring life's trials, and though we know we will have a grand reunion one day, we miss them here and now.

It's okay to mourn with the heavens from time to time. Solomon, the wisest man who ever lived, recognized there is a time to feel the sorrow of our losses, to miss those who no longer walk the earth with us. It's also comforting to know we *"will not grieve as the rest, who have no hope"* (1 Thessalonians 4:13) because we have eternal life. After a great loss, the healing slowly begins. Little by little, mourning succumbs to rejoicing, until Christ finally wipes every tear from our eyes.

Just as there is a time to mourn, there is a time to dance — to rejoice, to celebrate, and to let go of our cares. When we leave this earth, or Christ returns, our days of mourning will end forever. Heaven's gates will welcome us to a place of perfect life with our perfect Lord. The momentary trials we suffered on earth will pale in light of God's glory. We will have forever to rejoice in the wonder of all God prepared for us.

Weeping may last for the night, but a shout of joy comes in the morning.
(Psalm 30:5b, NASB1995)

DAY 1 | PRAY:

Despite these earthly sorrows, I will be glad and rejoice with all my heart, for you, Lord, have taken away my punishment and turned back my enemies. The Lord, the King of Israel, is with me. Never again will I fear any harm. (Zephaniah 3)

DAY 2 | MEMORIZE:

Revelation 21:4

And God will wipe away every tear from their eyes; there shall be no more death, nor sorrow, nor crying. There shall be no more pain, for the former things have passed away.

DAY 3 | READ AND RESPOND:

John 11:1-45

What was Jesus' initial response (verse 4) when He heard Lazarus was sick?

_____
_____
_____

How do we know Martha understood and believed in resurrection to eternal life?

_____
_____
_____

Why did Jesus weep, even though He knew Lazarus would soon be raised from death?

_____
_____
_____

Was God glorified through Lazarus' death and resurrection? Was there rejoicing? How do we know?

_____
_____
_____

DAY 4 | DO:

Think about one of the sorrowful moments in your life. Now think about one of the happiest. Note any insights God gives you into the transition from mourning to rejoicing or Lazarus being brought from death to life.

REFLECTIONS

DAY 5 | JOURNAL:

Record prayers, thoughts, or insights from your time with God.

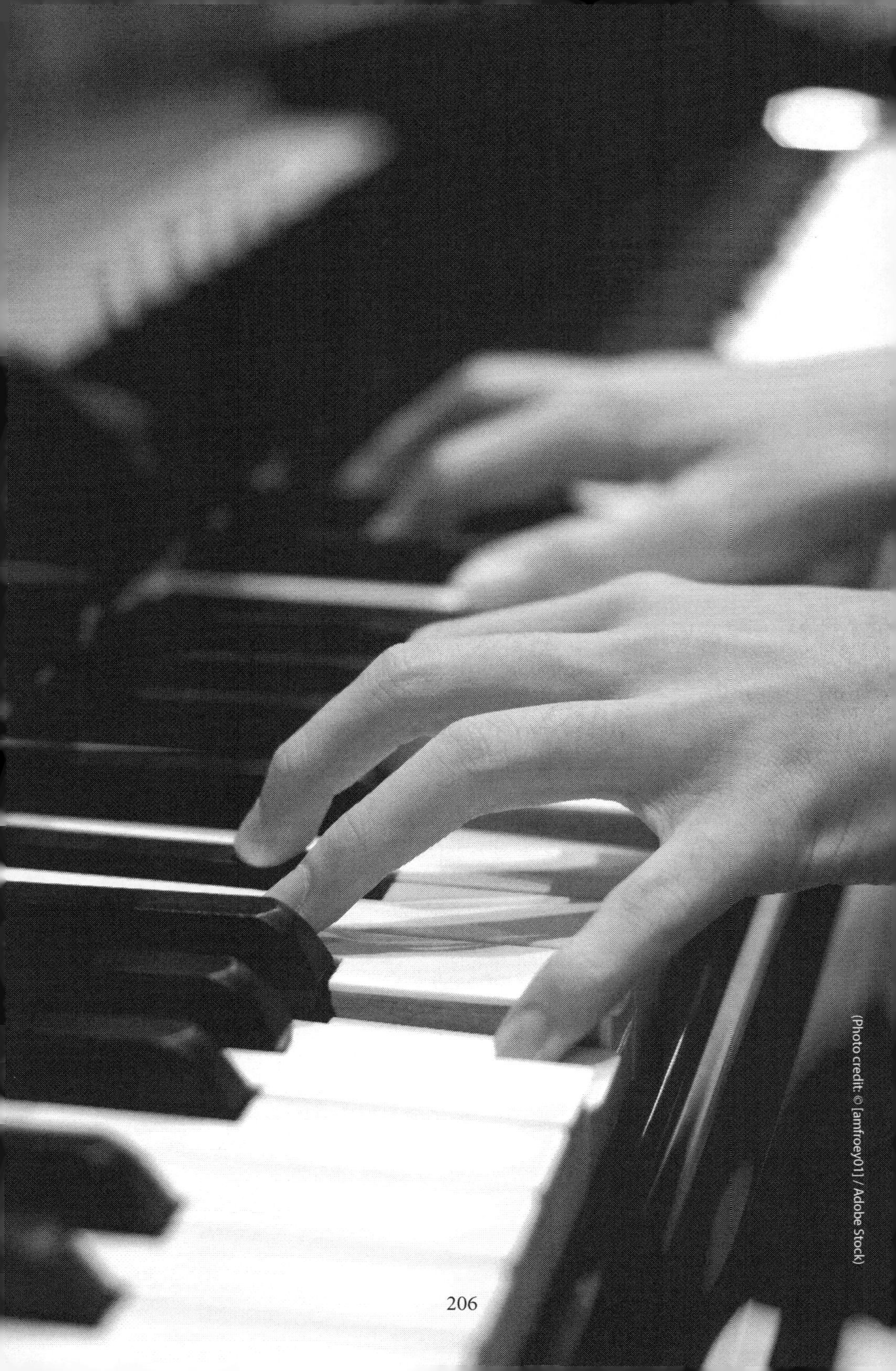
(Photo credit: © [amfroey01] / Adobe Stock)

JOURNEYING WITH SELF

WEEK 51: FROM DEFEAT TO TRIUMPH

CONSIDER:

Seventy hours. That's how long I sat at a piano keyboard and played, hoping to win the $1,000 grand prize. I was going to use the money toward a summer mission trip. When I first sat down, I had great hopes of winning. But as the hours ticked on, I felt defeat settling in. I was so tired, I could no longer remember what those little black dots on the page meant.

Seventy hours. Unfortunately, it wasn't long enough to win. I went home with nothing to show for my physical exhaustion and mental torment. The mission trip never happened because God had not ordained it.

I've lived through several other seasons of defeat since my walk with God began. I embarked on self-appointed ventures, with great hopes of victory. As I pushed on, I saw God closing the door on the horizon. In the end, I had nothing to show for my misadventures, except lessons learned about where true victory lies.

Think about David. He plotted a course to make Bathsheba his own, a course involving lust, deception, and murder. It seemed like a good idea to him at the time. It even worked! He got the girl. But she came at a high cost. In time, God redeemed the situation — when Solomon became king and built the temple.

Many sorrows shall be to the wicked; But he who trusts in the Lord, mercy shall surround him. (Psalm 32:10)

When God takes us down new paths, He goes before us, He goes with us, and He fights on our behalf. Pursuing God's will and purposes sets us up for triumph. There will still be battles. We may still come through physically exhausted and mentally tormented. But we will be victorious, by God's grace.

And the Lord, He is the One who goes before you. He will be with you, He will not leave you nor forsake you; do not fear nor be dismayed. (Deuteronomy 31:8)

Look at Job, a faithful man whom God allowed to undergo severe trials. Throughout Job's sufferings, God was near, hearing his cries for help, responding to his questions, and sustaining him until he proved himself true.

One day soon, our earthly defeats and victories will end. The door to our final triumph will stand open, with our Savior waiting to welcome us home. We can join Job in confidently declaring:

For I know that my Redeemer lives, and He shall stand at last on the earth; And after my skin is destroyed, this I know, that in my flesh I shall see God. (Job 19:25-26)

DAY 1 | PRAY:

Lord, you are the Alpha and the Omega, the Beginning and the End. You will freely give the water of life to all who thirst. All who overcome will inherit all things. You will be my God and I will be your child. Thank you, Lord! You give me the victory through my Lord Jesus Christ. (Revelation 21, 1 Corinthians 15)

DAY 2 | MEMORIZE:

2 Corinthians 2:14

Now thanks be to God who always leads us in triumph in Christ, and through us diffuses the fragrance of His knowledge in every place.

DAY 3 | READ AND RESPOND:

Revelation 3

What are Christ's accusations against the churches in Sardis and Laodicea?

Why does He commend the church in Philadelphia?

Which church best mirrors your own spiritual condition right now?

What does Christ promise to the overcomers in all three churches?

DAY 4 | DO:

Though the word "hell" never appears in the Bible, there are 162 references to eternal death and suffering in Scripture.

Follow this link: *https://www.openbible.info/topics/hell*.
Read a few of the verses and form a mental image of hell.

Now follow this link: *https://www.openbible.info/topics/heaven*.
Read a few of the verses and form a mental image of heaven.
Let God's truth compel you to tell those you love about God's free gift of salvation and the eternal triumph awaiting those who love Him.

REFLECTIONS

DAY 5 | JOURNAL:

Record prayers, thoughts, or insights from your time with God.

(Photo credit © [nataba] / Adobe Stock)

WEEK 52: FROM DISCOURAGEMENT TO HOPE

CONSIDER:

Around here, pussy willows are the first plant to "bloom." Tiny tufts of light gray fur peek out from their dark brown covers, like a litter of kittens clinging to a tree trunk. They thrive in the most unfriendly places, yet they embody happiness. Their cheerful appearance, their soft coats, and their earthy aroma are full of springtime promises.

Pussy willows take "bloom where you're planted" to heart. Every spring, despite their rather dismal surroundings, they put on a fine show. They don't let the stinky swamp water dampen their spirits. They don't complain that their feet are always wet. They aren't intimidated by the gang of tag alders crowding around them. And they don't wait around for the cattails to do their thing. They cheerfully do exactly what God has called them to do, exactly when they are called to do it, despite their circumstances.

Apart from Christ and a God-given purpose, life's circumstances can be downright discouraging. We have ongoing struggles — financially, relationally, spiritually. These quagmires threaten to rob us of our hope, our purpose, and our will to move forward with Christ. Rather than blooming where we're planted, we're tempted to wait for our circumstances to improve.

What if Esther had been discouraged? She was living in a home and married to a man she didn't choose, yet she used the status thrust upon her to save the Israelite people. At great personal risk, and with unwavering hope, she rose to the occasion and to Mordecai's challenge.

Yet who knows whether you have come to the kingdom for such a time as this? (Esther 4:14)

What if Joseph had fallen into despair? Sold into slavery, falsely accused, and forgotten in prison, he had every reason to wait for his circumstances to improve. But he faithfully, hopefully served God no matter where life took him. When at last he was reunited with his brothers, Joseph said:

As for you, you meant evil against me, but God meant it for good in order to bring about this present result, to preserve many people alive. (Genesis 50:20)

God has placed us in our circumstances with intent and purpose. Wherever life takes us, we can face our days with great hope rather than discouragement. The end of all our earthly struggles is our unseen reward above. The end of all our obedience to our earthly calling is our heavenly home in the eternal presence of our Savior and King.

DAY 1 | PRAY:

Lord, if I died with you, I shall also live with you. If I endure, I will also reign with you. You are my hope, O Lord God. I will hope continually and will praise you yet more and more. (2 Timothy 2, Psalm 71)

DAY 2 | MEMORIZE:

Hebrews 10:36

For you have need of endurance, so that after you have done the will of God, you may receive the promise.

DAY 3 | READ AND RESPOND:

Revelation 21

List the five things in this passage that give you the greatest hope.

1. _____

2. _____

3. _____

4. _____

5. _____

REFLECTIONS
_____
_____

DAY 4 | DO:

Draw a picture of or describe what you imagine the new heaven and new earth will be like.

DAY 5 | JOURNAL:

Record prayers, thoughts, or insights from your time with God.

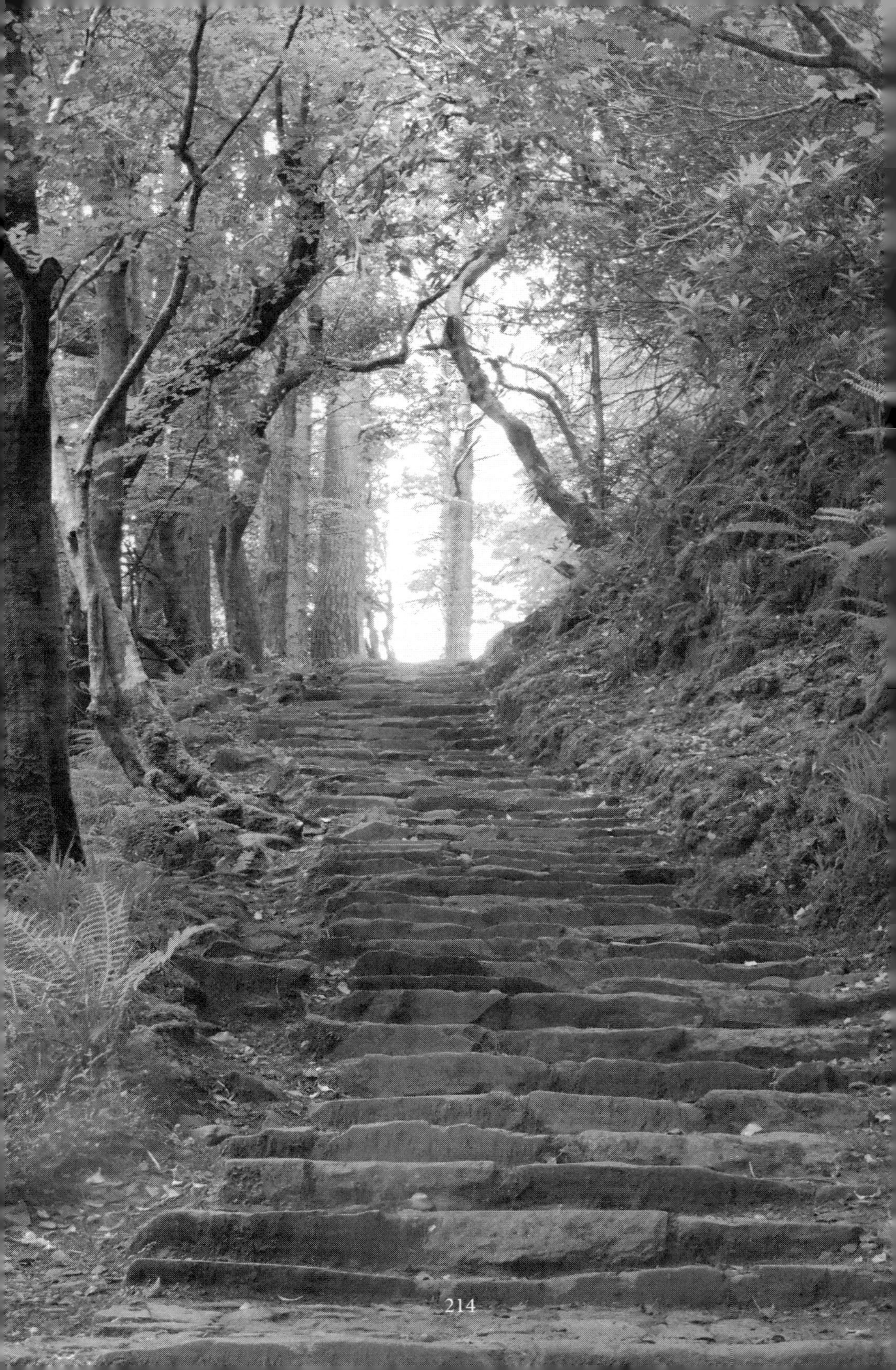

PARTING THOUGHTS

I pray all who read these pages will find hope and encouragement in them. At the end of 1 Thessalonians 4, Paul gives us a glimpse of Christ's return. There has been, and still is, much debate about what that will look like. The crucial point is not the details. The crucial point is Christ will return. He will come, bringing justice. He will come to fulfill His promises. He will come and put an end to darkness and evil.

Paul ends the chapter with this admonition: *"Therefore, comfort one another with these words."* The Lord *will* return! We *will* live in His presence *"in fullness of joy"* (Psalm 16:11) for eternity. We *will* be reunited with loved ones who belonged to God. We *will* be forever freed from the curse of sin and our mortal bodies. Despite the world around us, despite those who disappoint us, despite difficult circumstances, we have every reason to embrace hope. Let's comfort one another with God's promises of our eternal homecoming as we fix our eyes on Jesus, the author and perfector of our faith. (Hebrews 12:2)

Made in the USA
Monee, IL
08 November 2024

aac481fc-9516-48d3-8aed-cf984b05a9b0R01

One day life's journey will be over and you'll see your Savior face to face. Until then —
Blessings,
Michelle Adurrias